ACCIDENTAL
ARCHAEOLOGISTS

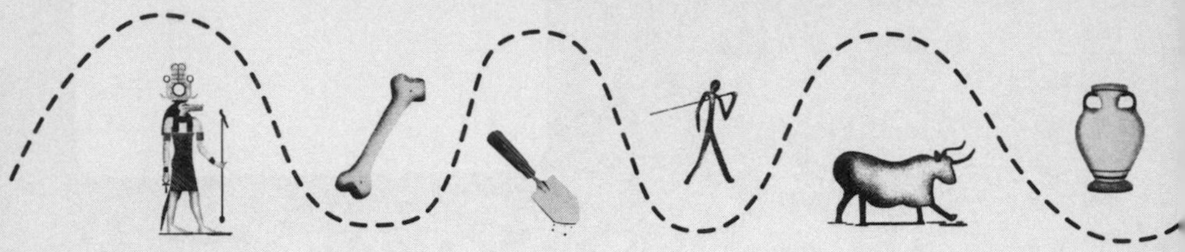

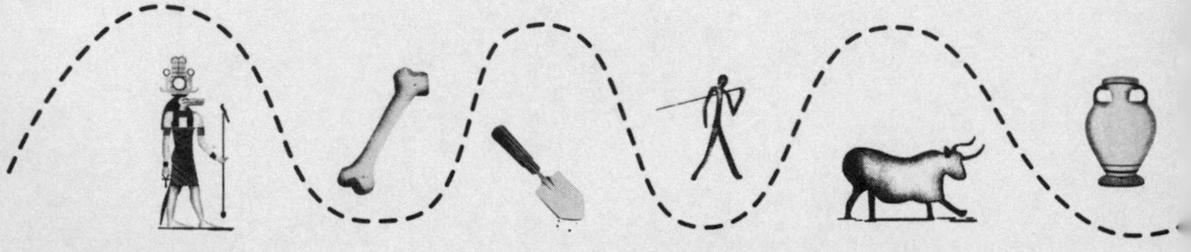

ACCIDENTAL ARCHAEOLOGISTS

TRUE STORIES OF
UNEXPECTED
DISCOVERIES

SARAH ALBEE

ILLUSTRATED BY
NATHAN HACKETT

Scholastic Press

Library of Congress Cataloging-in-Publication Data available

ISBN 978-1-338-57578-1 (paperback) / 978-1-338-57579-8 (hardcover)

1 2020

Printed in the U.S.A.   23

First edition, November 2020

Book design by Kay Petronio

CONTENTS

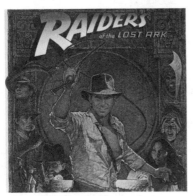

⇌ INTRODUCTION ⇌

A BUNCH OF AMATEURS

Dumb Luck and Happy Accidents

This is a book about chance discoveries by ordinary people that led to huge leaps in our knowledge of human history. These ordinary people included construction workers, farmers, soldiers, cave explorers, hikers, and yes, even kids. Most of them were just going about their day-to-day lives—digging a ditch, fixing a fence, searching for a lost goat—when they stumbled across an archaeological bonanza.

Before we proceed further, though, there's something you should know: Archaeological discoveries don't typically happen this way. Archaeology is a slow, deliberate, and careful field of study. Discoveries that make the news usually happen after years of painstaking work. So think of this book as an archaeological highlight reel.

Some of the ordinary, everyday people in this book found actual buried treasure—gold, jewels, and works of art. Others found stuff that you

Real-life archaeologists don't operate quite the same way that they do in movies.

and I would not describe as treasure but an archaeologist definitely would—a battered heap of metal, crumbling strips of papyrus, dusty old bones. Safe to say, if a discovery is included in this book, it has proven to be priceless, because it has changed what we thought we knew about the past.

The fossils, artifacts, and ancient human remains that the people in this book discovered have helped answer many questions. But they've also raised new ones.

It's okay not to have the answers. That's the point. In fact, the real goal of this book is to show you that while the past doesn't change, the stories we tell about the past *do* change. As new discoveries are made, archaeologists and historians continually reinterpret and reframe their perspectives on human history.

Another goal of this book is to encourage you to do some further digging. You may be inspired to grow up to study archaeology. Or you may decide to do more research about a particular historical period that interests you.

The Key Thing

Sometimes chance discoveries happen when the earth's surface is disturbed suddenly or unexpectedly, revealing a glimpse of something from the past that had been hidden. One archaeologist calls these sudden or unexpected glimpses "keyholes." A naturally occurring keyhole might be created by erosion, a fallen tree, or an earthquake. A human-made keyhole might be created by construction workers, well diggers, or farmers. An aerial keyhole can provide a new view from above. It shows anomalies on the earth's surface that had previously been undetectable by those at ground level.

In every one of the discoveries in this book, someone noticed something out of the ordinary. They looked, and then they saw— not always the same thing.

LET'S TALK TERMS

Before you dig in, it will help to review a few of these words, because you'll see a lot of them in this book.

Anomaly: In an archaeological sense, an anomaly is a part of a landscape that looks different or peculiar and that might have been altered by humans in the past. It could be a strange depression, an oddly shaped lump, or a flat-topped mound.

Anthropology: the study of people, both living and from the past, specifically their language, culture, and biology.

Archaeology: a branch of anthropology that studies the stuff left behind by humans who lived in the past. It includes things people built, used, or made, including pottery, artwork, buildings, or everyday items.

Artifact: something from the past that people left behind, especially an object that is of interest to an archaeologist. Usually artifacts are fairly portable, like a piece of pottery or a stone tool.

Feature: It's like an artifact, but bigger. A feature can be anything made by people, such as a road, building, or burial mound.

Fossil: the preserved remains of a once-living thing, usually found in the layers of the earth.

Paleoanthropology: the study of ancient humans and once-living humanlike relatives.

Chapter One

A BLAST FROM THE PAST

THE DiSCOVERY

The year is 1709. The place, a small fishing village in southern Italy, near Naples. A mountain called Vesuvius looms above the village. Local people have heard stories about the mountain that date back to the days of ancient Rome. They've heard that Vesuvius might be a volcano. According to those stories, the volcano had destroyed and buried some towns centuries ago, but no one has a clue as to the exact location of those ancient towns. The area around Vesuvius is now fertile farmland, where grapes and olive groves thrive.

On this day in 1709, some workmen are digging a well. Deep below the ground, they find some old and expertly cut pieces of marble. You'd think they'd say, "Aha! The ancient towns!" But on this day in 1709, no one puts two and two together.

A few years pass. The Spanish Bourbons now occupy this part of the Italian peninsula. The new ruler of the area is King Charles III. He's heard rumors about the marble that got dug up, and he enjoys redecorating as much as the next king, so he orders the digging to resume.

It soon becomes clear that the marble found in 1709 came from an ancient Roman amphitheater. Workers find more marble, and also beautiful Roman statues and other pieces of art.

King Charles VII of Naples (later known as King Charles III of Spain), posing cheerfully with a possibly plundered marble column.

Sure enough, they've rediscovered one of the ancient towns that had been destroyed back in 79 CE. It will later turn out to be a town once called Herculaneum (pronounced her-kyuh-LAY-nee-um). But no one especially cares about the history of what's down there. They just want to dig up the treasures. Workers—many of them forced laborers—dig tunnels haphazardly and carry off priceless Roman artifacts for the Spanish king's treasury. There's no archaeologist in sight. No attempt is made to note where things are found. No one records plans or maps or elevations. It's just a game of Finders Keepers.

More people hear of the discovery of the ancient town. In 1748 excavators find a second site about nine miles from Herculaneum. It will later be revealed as the town once called Pompeii. Under a thick layer of dust and ash, the excavators are surprised to find most of Pompeii is still in pretty good shape. Also, it's not buried as deeply as Herculaneum, so it's easier to uncover.

The foreigners are eventually driven out of Italy. Over the next hundred years or so, excavations at the site of Pompeii—and to a lesser extent the harder-to-reach Herculaneum—are conducted more carefully. Finally actual archaeologists take charge. Their goal is to learn about the ancient past rather than merely to plunder treasure.

The rest of the world begins to realize the magnitude of the discovery. Because the eruption of Vesuvius had happened unexpectedly and buried these towns relatively quickly, amazing details about life in ancient Rome have been preserved.

JUST BEFORE CATASTROPHE STRUCK

Back in 79 CE, Herculaneum was a fashionable seaside town on the bay of Naples, in the shadow of Mount Vesuvius. With about five thousand residents, Herculaneum was slightly smaller than the neighboring resort town of Pompeii, where wealthy people from Rome had built villas by the water to escape the hustle and bustle of Rome. Both towns were a mixture of wealthy Romans, middle-class shopkeepers and artisans, and poorer laborers and slaves.

The day began like many other days. Herculaneum's well-paved, well-drained streets thronged with people. Some went to the public baths. Others swam, or went to the ball courts to play games. The ball, called a *pila*, was made with an inflated animal bladder. Fountains burbled in the shady courtyards of fancy villas. In the town's center, people visited snack bars, dry cleaners, bakeries, and even public toilets.

AND THEN CATASTROPHE STRUCK

For the past few days, there'd been subtle warning signs. Mild tremors. Wells that had suddenly dried up. But no one paid much attention. Why would they?

Much of what we know about that terrible day comes from a writer named Pliny (PLIH-nee). He's known as Pliny the Younger to distinguish him from his uncle, the well-known writer of natural history named Pliny the Elder. Pliny the Younger was seventeen when Vesuvius erupted. He later wrote an account of the day, in two letters to his friend, the historian Tacitus.

At the time of the eruption, the younger Pliny lived with his mother and uncle in the town of Micenum, about twenty miles across the Bay of Naples from Herculaneum and Pompeii. The Pliny family had a perfect view of Vesuvius.

It happened around midday.

A sudden jolt. A tremendous blast. People on the streets of Herculaneum and Pompeii stopped and stared at the mountain. A giant column shot twelve miles into the air, where it bloomed into a mushroom-shaped cloud.

At their home across the bay, Pliny's mother roused her brother, the elder Pliny, from his studies to point out the window. A "cloud of unusual size and appearance" had emerged above the

A nighttime view of the eruption from across the Bay of Naples.

mountain. Today this kind of volcanic event is known as a Plinian eruption in honor of Pliny the Younger, because he wrote such an accurate account of it.

Events unfolded differently in Herculaneum than in Pompeii. On the day of the eruption, the winds were blowing toward Pompeii, which lay to the southeast of Vesuvius. Herculaneum was closer but was west of the mountain.

POMPEII

About thirty minutes after the eruption, a cloud of ash engulfed Pompeii. Pebbles of pumice[1] rained down on the town.

....

1   Pumice is a porous, lightweight rock that forms when steam-filled volcanic material cools off rapidly. It floats in water.

Alarm soon turned to panic. The bright sun disappeared, plunging the city into total darkness. Many townspeople fled to the countryside right away. Others took shelter inside their homes. For about eleven hours, it continued to "rain" pumice. The pellety precipitation wasn't heavy enough to hurt a person, but before long, roofs collapsed from the weight of the pumice and ash.

THE DATING GAME

Pliny's writings say that the eruption happened on August 24, 79 CE. But recent findings in the ruins of the towns of Pompeii and Herculaneum suggest that the eruption may, in fact, have happened in October. Clues in support of the October date include the clothing people were wearing, the existence of fruits such as pomegranates on tables (which aren't yet ripe in August but are in October), a coin that was found that seems to have been minted after August, and, most compellingly, some graffiti on a wall in Pompeii that appears to be dated October 17, 79 CE.

In the days before the printing press, ancient texts, including Pliny's letters, were copied and recopied by hand, so it's possible that someone copied down the wrong month at some point. We may find out more clues as new documents and artifacts are uncovered.

A majority of the inhabitants of Pompeii had time to escape—historians estimate there were about twenty thousand people in the town the day of the eruption. Those who died—about two thousand, we think—were killed either by falling rocks and caved-in roofs, or because they chose to remain in the town rather than flee, and were killed by the next horrifying phase of Mount Vesuvius's eruption. More on that soon.

HERCULANEUM

Because the wind was blowing away from Herculaneum, the city was mostly spared from the rain of pumice. People had more time to react and run away, so there were far fewer casualties. By midafternoon most people had fled the town.

HOW IT WENT DOWN

About twelve hours after the initial blast, the volcanic eruption shifted to its second phase, and this one proved far deadlier. At about one in the morning, the mushroom cloud of gas and molten debris that had shot so many miles into the sky above the volcano began to collapse. It happened in stages. With each partial collapse of the cloud, a surge of poisonous air blew down the slope, followed minutes later by a tidal wave of hot volcanic mud. It roared down the slope of the mountain faster than a speeding train. Scientists call this toxic cocktail of gas plus hot debris "pyroclastic surge and flow." Over seven hours, fiery clouds of gas and hot mud roared into Herculaneum. They buried the city and flash-seared anyone who'd remained behind. When it was over, the town lay under seventy-five feet of debris, which gradually hardened as it cooled. It sealed everything in a deep layer of rock—including bodies, wood, food, and everyday household objects.

Pompeii avoided the first few waves of pyroclastic surge and flow. One blanket of hot debris stopped just before the gates of the town. But by the morning after the eruption, a fourth, fifth, and sixth wave thundered into Pompeii. The massive surge of volcanic gas smothered the remaining people, and then quickly buried them in the flow.

PLINY THE ELDER

Pliny the Elder was a commander of the Roman navy. But he was also a scientist, and utterly fascinated by the events he was witnessing. He decided to sail across the bay and study the volcano up close. He invited his nephew to come along—what could be more fun than to sail straight toward an actively erupting volcano?—but the younger Pliny opted to stay home.

The elder Pliny set sail with a fleet of ships. Initially his plan was to record his observations, but he also went to rescue people stranded on the beach. The ships docked for the night at the town of Stabiae. The next day, Pliny the Elder collapsed and died, possibly from breathing the toxic fumes, or from a heart attack. His body was discovered on the beach two days later.

BEATING A RETREAT

By about eight thirty on the morning after the eruption, Pliny the Younger and his mother realized it was time to leave Micenum. The air had become "blacker and denser than any ordinary night." They joined a fleeing, panicked mob of people. "Broad sheets of fire and leaping flames" were still visible on the mountaintop. As Pliny described it, the "fearful black cloud" descended on the people of Micenum as they fled. "Many besought the aid of the gods, but still more imagined there were no gods left, and that the universe was plunged into eternal darkness for evermore." Pliny was sure they were all, quite literally, toast. But luckily for Pliny, and for history, the black cloud suddenly lifted. The sun emerged. He and his mother saw "everything changed, buried deep in ashes like snowdrifts."

REMAINS TO BE SEEN

In 1863 an Italian archaeologist named Giuseppe Fiorelli took over responsibility for the excavations. At the site of Pompeii, he discovered human-shaped empty spaces in the layers of ash that once held human bodies. The bodies had long since decayed away. Fiorelli realized that by filling the empty spaces with plaster, he could recreate the positions people (and animals) were in during their last anguished moments. The plaster forms have horrified and fascinated visitors to Pompeii ever since.

For a long time few signs of actual human remains were found in Herculaneum, which led archaeologists to assume that nearly everyone had escaped. But in the 1980s, another accidental

Haunting plaster casts of two victims from Pompeii, in their final moments.

archaeological find occurred. As workers installed a drainage pipe near the area of the ancient shoreline, they uncovered some human skeletons. Eventually more than three hundred would be found. Archaeologists now believe that a group of Herculaneans who hoped to flee by sea had taken refuge in boathouses, waiting to be rescued by ships. But they had been killed by the pyroclastic flow. Some of the people died frozen in an embrace.

Besides the human skeletons, archaeologists uncovered wood, cloth, delicate glassware, and even food. These everyday household items have helped form a vivid snapshot of a typical day in an ancient Roman town.

BACK TO THE PRESENT

Modern-day tourists can stroll the streets of Pompeii and Herculaneum, walk inside the houses, and even read the graffiti on the walls.

Excavation continues, but it's complicated. Exposed wall

paintings fade in the light, and unearthed structures are subject to erosion and deterioration. Pigeons roost in buildings and peck away at wooden beams. Archaeologists ended large-scale open-air excavations at Pompeii in the 1960s, because they worried about the possibility of further decay. Keeping stuff buried actually helps protect it.

Today the horror of what happened on that day in 79 CE has become much better understood. Archaeologists have uncovered more and more details about the way these ancient townspeople lived—and how they died.

And it's thanks to Pliny the Younger that we know so much about the sequence of the eruption. Scientists who study volcanoes are amazed at the detailed way he described each phase of the catastrophe and how well his account correlates with modern-day information about volcanoes. Pliny himself didn't realize the significance of what he'd so accurately reported. "Of course," he wrote, "these details are not important enough for history."

Chapter Two

ETCHED IN STONE

THE DISCOVERY

The year is 1799. The place, a small village in northern Egypt. Egyptians call it Rashid. The French call it Rosette.

What French people call it is relevant here because the French army has recently invaded Egypt. France and Britain are at war. Again. And Egypt, with its central location, turns out to be a popular destination for warring Europeans interested in controlling the territories around the Mediterranean Sea.

On this day French soldiers are strengthening the foundations of a crumbling old fort. The fort was built by Ottoman Turks back in the fifteenth century, with stones looted from nearby ancient Egyptian sites. For centuries, the ruins of many of Egypt's temples have been pillaged for building stones by whoever happens to occupy the country.

The French soldiers' commander is Napoleon Bonaparte. Perhaps you've heard about him. In 1799 he's not yet the most powerful ruler in the world. He's still just a general, but he's catapulting up

Napoleon in Egypt, posing with the Sphinx.

the ranks of power faster than you can say "emperor-to-be."

Meanwhile, back at the fort, an ordinary soldier named D'Hautpoul stumbles across a dark-gray slab of granite. It has curious-looking writing carved into it. He alerts his commander, Pierre-Francoise Bouchard. Bouchard realizes right away that this is one valuable hunk of rock. They dig it out. The stone

The Rosetta stone.

is about the size of a car door, but a whole lot heavier—almost a ton,[1] to be exact.

Although no one yet knows it, this stone slab is going to be the

1   A ton is two thousand pounds. That's more than a large cow weighs, and twice as heavy as a grand piano.

key to unlocking an entire ancient civilization. It will soon become known as the Rosetta stone.

THE BRAINS OF THE OPERATION

In the decades leading up to the French invasion of Egypt, Europeans had been making rapid advancements in the study of history, science, philosophy, and government. It was a period we now call the Age of Enlightenment. Like many Europeans at the time, Napoleon was fascinated by ancient Egypt and interested in gathering knowledge about it. So in addition to soldiers, he also brought to Egypt dozens and dozens of biologists, mineralogists, linguists, mathematicians, chemists, and assorted other scientists. He wanted to prove that French scholars were the greatest thinkers in the world. Their job was to unlock the secrets of this mysterious country, and to study, measure, sample, and, when possible, seize all the important cultural artifacts they could get their hands on, so that the artifacts could be shipped back to France.

French scholars, artists, and scientists in Egypt, who probably sweltered in their impractical European clothing.

Nowadays it's extremely unethical to take cultural artifacts from their country of origin, and in many places it's downright illegal (see "A Little More Dirt on Archaeology," page 186). But Napoleon was not the sort of guy to be burdened by his conscience. In his mind, the more discoveries and treasures his team of French scholars could uncover and ship back home, the more they would boost France's prestige around the world. By which he meant *Napoleon's* prestige.

MILITARY MESS-UP

The first month in Egypt had gone pretty well for Napoleon's armies. Egypt was still part of the Ottoman Empire and was ruled by warriors called Mamluks, who fought fiercely and feared no enemy. So when the French arrived, the Mamluks were waiting for them. The French won the first battle, now known as the Battle of the Pyramids. But things took a distinct turn for the worse for Napoleon and his troops when Napoleon learned that the British admiral Horatio Nelson had sunk most of the French fleet anchored off the coast of Egypt. Soon after that Napoleon marched his troops into Syria and staged an unsuccessful siege of a walled city called Acre. The French army was forced to retreat, and went back to Egypt. Napoleon found himself marooned in Egypt with 35,000 soldiers, and his men were dying from plague. To make a grumpy future dictator even grumpier, Napoleon pined for the woman he'd recently married, Josephine. He'd been writing her lovey-dovey letters ever since they'd parted, and he'd even sent her bits and parts of several mummies, as a token of his esteem. Because nothing says I love you like a shriveled head.

But while the military campaign was going badly, the scholars made big strides. They set up chemistry labs and collected botanical specimens. They sketched and painted ancient temples, tombs, and monuments. They had developed new kinds of water pumps and produced detailed maps of Egypt. They'd even made pencils from melted-down lead bullets.

RETREAT AND DEFEAT

About a month after the Rosetta stone was discovered, Napoleon quietly skedaddled out of Egypt. He abandoned what was left of his sickly army, and all of the scholars he'd brought along. He rushed back to France, which was still reeling from its recent revolution. He believed France was primed to be taken over by whoever was on the spot to seize power. Napoleon had decided that he was just the right man for the job.

He left instructions for a general to take charge in Egypt, but that general died. So in 1801, a junior commander signed terms of surrender to the British. Included in the terms was a promise to hand over all the collections, notes, and artifacts that had been amassed by the French scholars. After many of the scholars protested, the British victors ultimately allowed them to keep their collections. All except the Rosetta stone. *That* the British were not about to give up. It was sent to London.

No one said trying to conquer the entire world would be easy.

CRACKING THE CODE

The stone, which had been carved in 196 BCE, is a fragment of a larger slab. It has an inscription that says the same thing in three different ancient languages. The first language is hieroglyphic, which no one in Napoleon's time knew how to read. It was the script used by ancient Egyptians for important or religious notices. It's a form of writing that looks like it's all pictures—kind of like ancient Egyptian emojis. The second language on the stone is demotic, which was the "everyday" kind of written language in ancient Egypt. The third is Greek: That was the language of the rulers of Egypt at the time the stone was carved.

Scholars realized right away that the Rosetta stone was their key to decoding hieroglyphics. But it took decades to figure out how the language worked. Two scholars, one British, one French, emerged as the most likely to decode the stone. It became a matter of national pride as to whether France or England would be the first to figure it out.

Scholars had their work cut out for them, trying to decipher hieroglyphics.

The British scholar Thomas Young made a major breakthrough in 1814 when he discovered that circles drawn around symbols (what the French called cartouches), represented people's names. Rule, Britannia!

Then the French scholar, Jean-Francois Champollion, made another huge discovery, in 1822. Champollion could read both ancient Greek and Coptic. He guessed Coptic was similar to Demotic. He guessed right. After years of studying the stone, he made a major mental leap and grasped that hieroglyphics are both pictures of words *and* sounds of the language. He looked at how certain signs were used in the Demotic language and was able to connect the signs to their hieroglyphic equivalents. The day he discovered that, he raced to his brother's office, burst in, and announced, "I've got it!" Then he fainted with excitement. Vive La France!

Champollion for the win!

A MUNDANE MESSAGE

So what does the inscription say? It's basically an official memo, written by Egyptian priests, that thanks the thirteen-year-old pharaoh, Ptolemy V, for reducing taxes . . . on Egyptian priests. Similar tablets were put into every other temple in Egypt, so the message was really nothing special back in its day. But it's pretty special to us. Think about *that* next time you write a thank-you note to your great-aunt Sharon for the itchy sweater she gave you. Your note just might be found and deciphered two thousand years from now.

BACK TO THE PRESENT

The French have been annoyed that the British held on to the Rosetta stone all these years, but the people who *really* have a right to be annoyed are the Egyptians. There's a strong argument to be made that the stone rightly belongs to them. In 2003 the Egyptian government asked the British Museum to return the stone to its original home—Egypt.

Officials at the British Museum—probably after they'd stopped rolling on the floor laughing—politely said no. But the museum did make a copy of the stone for the Egyptians in 2005. The Egyptians have continued to request the return of the stone. Perhaps one day it will be restored to its rightful place.

Today the Rosetta stone remains on display at the British Museum.

Chapter Three

A GiANT
IN THE FiELD

THE DiSCOVERY

The year is 1814. The place is London, England. In front of a boisterous crowd, the Great Belzoni steps onto the stage. It's time for the act everyone has been waiting for. It's called . . .

THE HUMAN PYRAMID!

Giovanni Belzoni is six feet, seven inches tall. He's handsome and well proportioned, with broad shoulders and bulging muscles. As he struts to center stage, wearing tinsels, feathers, and scanty tights, more than one young lady probably fans herself. The crowd holds its collective breath.

Let's let an awed eyewitness describe what happens next: "He clasps round a belt to which are fixed ledges to support the men

Sig.º Belzoni. the Patagonian Sampson as he appeared at Sadlers Wells
Theatre, Se...   1819...

R.H. Norman del.ⁿ

The Great Belzoni performing onstage, as depicted by an artist from
the time. We're pretty sure the people he lifted were average-size.

who cling round him, and first takes up one under each arm, receives one on either side, one on each of his shoulders, and one on his back, the whole forming a kind of Pyramid, when thus encumbered he moves as easy and graceful as if about to walk a minuet; and displays a flag in as flippant a manner as a dancer on the rope."

The crowd roars in approval.

Belzoni does move nimbly for a man of his immense size. If he'd been born in the twenty-first century, he would probably have been a first-round draft pick for the NBA. But this being 1814, he's balancing ten adults on his back to form a human pyramid.

A year later the Great Belzoni will find himself in the land of actual, ancient pyramids—Egypt. And he'll become an accidental archaeologist.

FOUNTAINS OF YOUTH

Giovanni Battista Belzoni was born in 1778 in Padua, Italy. His father was a barber. His mother suffered from chronic headaches, possibly due to having given birth to four supersized boys but also because her husband's meager income had to be stretched to support a houseful of aunts, cousins, brothers-in-law, and grandchildren. When Giovanni was sixteen, to lessen the burden on his weary parents, he left home for good and headed to Rome to seek his fortune.

Details of his time in Rome are sketchy. He may have worked as a fountain repairman. But while the location was good—there are a lot of fountains in Rome—his timing was terrible. Napoleon's army had taken over much of Europe, and Italy was next. In 1798 the French marched into Rome. Belzoni hoofed it out of the city.

HE MEETS HiS MATCH

He traveled through Europe, and in 1803 he arrived in England, where he eventually found work as a performer in various theaters and traveling road shows. He also met and married a woman named Sarah Barre. In time he developed his act and became known as the Great Belzoni.

For nine years the couple stayed in Britain, due to restrictions on traveling abroad during England's war with Napoleon. They traveled from town to town, and Belzoni performed his act. During that time, he perfected a unique skill set: He could lift huge weights, use levers and rollers, and balance large loads.

A CHANCE ENCOUNTER

In 1812 the Napoleonic Wars finally began to wind down. Belzoni and Sarah were at last free to leave England. They traveled through Europe and eventually arrived at an island in the Mediterranean called Malta. Unemployed and short on cash, Belzoni searched for work. One day he happened to meet an agent of the Pasha Muhammed Ali, the Turkish ruler who

A Pasha is a high-ranking ruler.

controlled Egypt. The agent recruited talent for the Pasha, who was interested in modernizing Egypt. He invited Belzoni to Egypt. Belzoni leapt at the opportunity to use his engineering skills.

He and Sarah arrived in Cairo in 1815, where Belzoni got to work building a hydraulic wheel, which he believed would modernize outmoded ways to irrigate farmers' crops.

But the Pasha's inner circle of advisors had no interest in Europeans and their "modernizing" innovations, and the demonstration flopped. All seemed lost, until the charming, handsome Belzoni struck up an acquaintance with the new British consul-general in Egypt, a snobby, ambitious man named Henry Salt. Salt had been told by his bosses back in England to collect as many Egyptian antiquities as he could and send them back to furnish the Egyptian wing of the British Museum. And Belzoni, who in Salt's eyes was a muscle-bound lunkhead, was the perfect guy to do all the heavy lifting.

Salt offered the strongman his first assignment: Belzoni was to figure out how to transport a colossal, seven-ton head-and-shoulders granite statue of Ramses II from Thebes (part of modern-day Luxor, Egypt) to Cairo—a distance of about three hundred miles. From there, it would be sent by ship to the British Museum.

Belzoni knew a thing or two about lifting huge weights, and he thought like an engineer, with a keen intuition and excellent problem-solving skills. Also, he really needed a job. So he readily agreed.

HEADS UP

Belzoni, with Sarah in tow, arrived in Thebes and contemplated his task. First, the enormous statue had to be transported overland two miles, from where it lay in a tomb, to the banks of the Nile.

Belzoni rounded up dozens of laborers. He directed them to lift the stone millimeter by millimeter, first one side, and then the other. Workers lodged four logs under the statue, one log at a time, to act as rollers. Then workers pulled the statue on ropes while others moved the rollers from the back to the front as the procession crept forward. In two days, they moved the statue two hundred yards. This was July. In the Sahara Desert.

At one point the massive load sank into the sandy desert soil and they had to take a three-hundred-yard detour. But five days later they'd dragged the statue to the bank of the river. Then they loaded it onto a boat en route for Cairo.

Belzoni and Sarah fell in love with Egypt, so they stayed. The strongman, usually as Salt's employee, traipsed around Egypt and

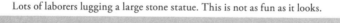

Lots of laborers lugging a large stone statue. This is not as fun as it looks.

located some of the most beautiful tombs ever to have been discovered. He found the entrance to the central chamber of one of the colossal pyramids at Giza. He traveled by camel caravan across the eastern Sahara to locate the ruins of the ancient port town called Berenice on the Red Sea. And he lugged a lot of loot out of Egypt and onto boats bound for Britain.

OCCUPATIONAL HAZARDS

Looting a country's cultural heritage was hard work, especially in Egypt. Temperatures often soared over 120 degrees Fahrenheit. Belzoni once got his huge shoulders wedged into a narrow passage inside a tomb and had to be dislodged by his guides. Another time, while traveling through the desert, Belzoni's camel stumbled and then fell on him, breaking several of his ribs. He was carried to the home of a local sheik, where it took him days to recover.

Another time, he took on a new assignment: to excavate and then transport a huge obelisk.[1] To get it onto a boat, workers built a ramp made of rocks. But as they dragged the obelisk across it, the ramp crumbled, and as Belzoni would later report, the priceless obelisk "majestically descended into the river." Somehow the Great Belzoni managed to fish it back out again, and this time they got it on board.

■ ■ ■

----

1   An obelisk is a tall stone column with a pointy top.

A pair of Egyptian obelisks where they belong—in Egypt.

FREE FOR ALL

In the early nineteenth century, Egypto-mania struck Europe. People suddenly took an interest in ancient Egypt's mysterious and long-forgotten past. More and more Europeans arrived to hunt for antiquities. Some were true scholars. Others were fortune hunters whose prime goal was to plunder tombs and sell artifacts back home at hugely inflated prices. Many of the early archaeologists, Belzoni among them, were somewhere in between.

Whether you see Belzoni as a tomb robber or as someone with a sincere interest in teaching the world about Egypt's past, there's no disputing that what he did required enormous physical stamina, courage, and management skills. But he sometimes employed highly questionable practices, by today's standards. Where modern archaeologists take great pains to uncover artifacts slowly and deliberately, with small hand tools and delicate brushes, Belzoni was less subtle. He used battering rams to bash open sealed tombs. He carved his name into walls and statue bases, so others would know he'd been the first to discover them.

He clambered across piles of mummies, squashing bodies and splintering bones, and he thought nothing of raiding treasures that had been sent with the dead to the afterlife. In his five years in Egypt, Belzoni uncovered tombs all over Upper Egypt and Nubia. He plundered everything from papyrus,[2] to mummies, to huge obelisks and sarcophagi.[3]

Belzoni was a product of his time. That's what everyone else was doing, too. Indifferent rulers cared little about the artifacts from thousands of years in the past. Corrupt tribal leaders were easily bribed, and impoverished villagers sold the mummies, papyrus rolls, and stone statues to whoever was willing to pay the most for them. Much of what Belzoni uncovered is now in the British Museum and other museums around Europe. The big loser was Egypt. Its treasures were ransacked by the French in the eighteenth century, and then by the British in the nineteenth; these foreigners carried away everything that wasn't nailed down.

....

2   Papyrus is a plant that grew all over the place in ancient Egypt. It's also the name of the material made from the plant, which was used by people in the ancient world to write on, before paper was invented. For more on papyrus, see page 38.

3   *Sarcophagi* is the plural of *sarcophagus*, which is a fancy coffin in which ancient Egyptians stashed the mummified remains of important people.

MUMMY FOR THE TUMMY

Mummy pits were simple grave sites for ordinary Egyptians from antiquity, whose mummies were stacked in tombs by the dozen. In Belzoni's day, some local people made a ghoulish living in the mummy market. They collected mummies and ground them into dust to be used as medicine. As early as the twelfth century, mummy powder had been considered an important cure-all for every sort of ailment. Mummy elixir was still popular in Belzoni's day.

BACK TO BRITAIN

Belzoni never felt accepted as a true archaeologist by the "gentlemen" in the profession. He was keenly aware that Salt and others treated him as the "paid help," and he felt that others took credit for his work. (Salt's name appears on most of the Belzoni-excavated Egyptian artifacts in the British Museum today.) Belzoni and Sarah left Egypt and returned to England in 1819. A year later he published a lengthy memoir about his travels, in which he endeavored to settle the score with his rivals and to recount his adventures. It sold like hotcakes. He became a celebrity.

Belzoni's name, carved into yet another priceless piece of antiquity.
Can you see Salt's name, too?

THE FINAL CHAPTER

The last chapter of Belzoni's *Narrative* is written by Sarah
and is called "Mrs. Belzoni's Trifling Account of the
Women of Egypt, Nubia, and Syria." It's a fascinating recap
of her own travels and presents a rare view of everyday life
of women in Egypt and Palestine. As Belzoni's wife, Sarah
made unique connections with women, usually the wives of
local officials. Sarah Belzoni lived to a ripe old age.

LAST TRIP

Belzoni enjoyed his celebrity status in England for a few years, but fame alone didn't pay his bills. He headed back to Africa, this time to locate the source of the river Niger. But that did not happen. He died of dysentery on his way to Timbuktu in 1823. He was forty-five years old.

BACK TO THE PRESENT

Today the Egyptian artifacts Belzoni excavated can be seen in museums all over Europe, including England, Italy, Germany, and France. Ever the showman, Belzoni helped generate huge enthusiasm and interest in ancient Egypt, and his discoveries continue to spark interest to this day.

Chapter Four

IN A PILE, CROCODILE

THE DISCOVERY

The year is 1899. The place, Lower Egypt. A man is surrounded by crocodiles.

You'd think he'd be frightened. Nile crocodiles (*Crocodylus niloticus*) can grow as long as a giraffe is tall. They can spring out of the muddy water with shocking speed. They've surprised many a villager, and not in a fun way. But this man is not frightened; he's annoyed. Because these crocodiles aren't alive. They're extremely dead. In short, they are two-thousand-year-old mummies.

Ancient Egyptians regularly mummified sacred animals. They worshipped cats, for instance. When a pet cat died, they often had it mummified. In this area of Egypt, in the ancient city of Tebtunis, the sacred animal of choice had been the crocodile.

Mediterranean Sea

LIBYA

Alexandria · Damietta · Port Said

CAIRO · Suez

SINAI

· Siwa

Tebtunis

SAUDI ARABIA

EGYPT

Nile

Luxor

Red Sea

Aswan

Lake Nasser

"Lower Egypt" refers to the northern part of the country and "Upper Egypt" refers to the southern part.

Dead crocodiles were mummified and left as offerings for a god named Sobek. Besides being the god of crocodiles, Sobek was also the god who protected you from the dangers of the Nile River (for instance, from crocodiles).

This site contains thousands of crocodiles, from mummified eggs to mummified baby crocodiles to mummified full-grown, nine-foot-long behemoths. But the man is not interested in crocodile mummies. He is looking for something else: papyrus.

The man is not an archaeologist. He's a local Egyptian guy, probably in his early twenties, or perhaps even a teenager. While his name has been lost to history, the two Englishmen who have employed him—Bernard Grenfell and Arthur Hunt—are already well known in archaeological circles.

Sobek, the crocodile god.

Grenfell and Hunt, looking excited about their crocodile jackpot.

Their instructions to this man and to his fellow workers are to look for ancient papyrus. Ideally, *rolls* of papyrus, although Grenfell and Hunt would settle for some scraps that are in decent condition. They want papyrus because it may contain rare ancient text. But all anyone is finding are mummified crocodiles.

Suddenly the man spots a large-ish mound. Is it a buried sarcophagus? Sometimes important people were sent to the afterlife with rolls of papyrus inside their sarcophagi so they'd have something interesting to read on their journey into the next world. Or religious texts would be included to help the dead person get to the afterlife, kind of like a passport.

But it's a false alarm. No sarcophagus. When he digs a bit more, he finds yet another row of crocodiles. In disgust, the man picks one up and flings it out of the way. The mummified animal breaks into several pieces.

Everyone stops.

Everyone gapes.

Inside the broken crocodile body, everyone can see that the animal has been stuffed with . . . papyrus.

CROCODILE FILES

The papyrus-stuffed mummy was a major discovery. Suddenly the excavation team became much more interested in the thousands of crocodile mummies they'd dug up and—probably—kicked to the side. Like frenzied children on Christmas morning, they unwrapped every crocodile mummy in sight. Most of the crocodiles turned out to contain no papyrus. They were stuffed with reeds and sticks and wrapped with linen cloth. But about 2 percent of them did contain it. Some of the larger animals had been wrapped in papyrus rolls several yards in length. Smaller sheets were found stuffed into their body cavities. The text written on these dated back to the second and first centuries BCE. This was the second time Grenfell and Hunt had hit the papyrus jackpot.

THE FIRST BIG FIND

Grenfell and Hunt's first papyrus jackpot happened two years before the Tebtunis papyri discoveries. They had organized a dig

GREEKS iN EGYPT

Alexander the Great, a Macedonian leader of Greece, conquered Egypt in 331 BCE. So for about three centuries after that, a whole line of Greek-speaking pharaohs ruled Egypt—most of whom belonged to a dynasty called the Ptolemies. Cleopatra is the most famous—and also the last—of the Ptolemaic pharaohs. When she died in 30 BCE, the Romans took control of Egypt, and Egypt became something of a multicultural hot spot. That explains why papyri that were uncovered in Tebtunis, and in other ancient Egyptian tombs and dumpsites, were in lots of different ancient languages, including Greek, Latin, Hieroglyphic, Hebrew, Coptic, Syriac, Aramaic, Arabic, Nubian, and early Persian.

at another site in Egypt. It was in the ruins of an ancient city called Oxyrhynchus, which means "town of the sharp-snouted fish."

There Grenfell and Hunt—or rather, their workers—found a huge trove of ancient Greek and Roman rolls of papyrus at the town dump. The find included a lot of stuff most people might think is boring, but which is not a bit boring to a papyrologist[1]—such as ancient tax receipts, recipes for indigestion, and horoscopes. And about 10 percent of the documents had been truly spectacular finds—literary masterpieces written by ancient Greek writers such as the philosopher Aristotle, the playwrights Sophocles and Euripides, and the poet Sappho (see pages 39–41). There were even fragments of Homer's epic poem *The Iliad.* The texts had all been handwritten on rolls of papyrus, some from as far back as the third century BCE.

Egyptians— the ones who did the actual work— searching for papyrus.

ROLL WITH IT

Papyrus was the go-to paper of the ancient world and a big improvement on clay tablets. It was made from the fibers of a reed, *Cyperus papyrus*, which once thrived in marshy areas along the banks of the Nile.

To make papyrus, Egyptians cut strips from the stalks and

....
1   A scientist who studies ancient rolls of papyrus. Most papyrologists know how to read some very cool ancient languages.

laid them out crossways, with one layer running vertically and another horizontally. Then they smooshed the layers tightly. The sap in the papyrus bound the layers together. The sheets were left out to dry. Then they were joined end to end to form a long strip, and pasted together with a solution of flour, water, and vinegar. Finally the seams were sanded smooth with seashells or ivory.

A roll could be about a foot high and as long as one hundred feet.

THE WRITTEN WORD

The printing press was invented around 1439.[2] Everything written before that had to be copied out by hand. In ancient Egypt, this tedious task fell to scribes. Scribes sat cross-legged on the ground, their papyrus laid across their laps, and copied out text. Their pens were made of a kind of reed, dipped into ink that was a mixture of soot, gum arabic (a sticky stuff from trees), and water. Scribes laid out the text in columns, sometimes numbered along the top. To produce multiple copies at once, a group of scribes would sit in a circle and take dictation from one person who read out loud.

A scribe and a scroll.

....

2   Although Chinese monks were setting text with block printing six hundred years before that. And the Chinese invented actual paper about 100 BCE.

REUSED AND RECYCLED

Papyrus wasn't very durable, and papyrus scrolls didn't last very long. But worn-out papyrus was too precious to throw away. It was usually recycled and reused. For instance, it might be stuffed inside a mummified crocodile to help it maintain its shape. Or it might be entirely repurposed and used to make a sarcophagus.

Because wood is scarce in the desert, ancient Egyptians formed mummy cases using a papier-mâché-like process. They pasted layers of recycled papyrus together with plaster. Then they molded sheets of this plastered-up old papyrus into the shape of mummy cases. Archaeologists call smooshed-up papyrus wads "cartonnage." The outer layer of the sarcophagus was smoothed over and painted.

Grenfell and Hunt were among the first archaeologists to discover valuable bits of papyrus used as cartonnage. Ever since, papyrologists have experimented with all kinds of ways of separating wadded-together clumps of cartonnage in order to be able to read the scraps of papyrus. Some methods worked better than others.

One of the most famous writers of ancient times whose work has been discovered in mummy cartonnage was the Greek poet Sappho.

PUZZLING PiECES

We don't have a lot of information about Sappho's personal life, but we know that she was one of the most admired poets of ancient Greece.

Sappho was born sometime in the first half of the seventh century BCE (possibly 610-ish BCE), and came from the Greek island called Lesbos. She was what's known as a lyric poet. Her poetry was composed to be sung—literally while strumming a lyre.

A nineteenth-century artist's fanciful idea of what Sappho may have looked like.

There are all kinds of stories about her life that we can't confirm. She might have married. She might have had a daughter. Her husband might have died. She might have fallen in love with both men and women. A thousand or so years after her death, in medieval Europe, this last possibility would horrify church officials, who would do their best to destroy whatever poems of hers they could find.

Sappho's life has been an endless source of fascination for artists over the centuries. There are dozens of paintings that show her in thoughtful poses, hair flowing, her very un-Greek-like dress tumbling off one shoulder and exposing her snow-white bosom. As if. Greek men did a lot of parading around naked at the gym, but "respectable" Greek women were expected to remain demurely wrapped in their *peploi*.[3]

....

3   *Peploi* is plural for *peplos*, which was a long, tubelike, wraparound garment worn by Greek women.

What we *can* know is that she wrote beautiful poems that talk of love and heartache and getting old, with a directness and clarity that packs a wallop even across the span of two thousand years. Although she was thought to have produced nine book-scrolls' worth of poetry (as many as ten thousand lines), only one complete poem of hers exists today (thanks, medieval church officials!). The rest of what has been found is only about six hundred fragmented lines, and some of the fragments had been used as mummy cartonnage that papyrologists painstakingly unstuck and reassembled. Grenfell and Hunt found six pieces of papyrus that contained parts of about eight of her poems. Since then, fragments of a few other Sappho poems have come to light—some as recently as 2012.

BACK TO THE PRESENT

Between 1896 and 1907, the teams of workers excavating on behalf of Grenfell and Hunt discovered enormous amounts of papyrus. Thousands of the fragments seemed in hopelessly terrible condition—blackened, worm-eaten, decayed, utterly illegible. But there's hope! Today, many major museums and universities have huge stashes of papyrus, ready to be pieced together and translated. Thanks to new technologies, papyrologists can now see texts that have become faded and darkened and unreadable to the naked eye. One new photographic technique, developed from satellite imaging, allows some of the faded ink, invisible under regular light, to come into view under infrared lighting.

The work is far from finished. By some estimates, only 1 to 2 percent of what may be as many as half a million papyrus fragments stored in universities and museums has been saved and cataloged. The remaining 98 percent still needs to be pieced together, deciphered, and analyzed.

Papyrologists expect that in this 98 percent they'll find previously unseen works by ancient masters like Sophocles and Aeschylus. They think it's likely they'll find more two-thousand-year-old biblical texts. And, we hope, more lines from Sappho. There's lots more work to do, and they'll need a lot of help. Maybe you should consider studying a few ancient languages. Think how fun you'd be at parties!

Chapter Five

WHAT A WRECK

THE DISCOVERY

The year is 1900. The place, a sea called the Aegean (pronounced uh-JEE-uhn), which is part of the eastern end of the Mediterranean Sea. Greek sponge fishermen from the island of Symi are sailing toward their fishing grounds when they suddenly encounter strong winds. They steer their boat to a sheltered area off the coast of a tiny island called Antikythera (an-tee-KIH-thee-ruh) for a few days. It's between Crete and the Greek mainland.

While they wait out the winds, they decide—why not?—to dive overboard to see if there are any sponges.[1] A diver plunges

....

1 The sponge you use to wipe your kitchen counter is a synthetic sponge. Those have been around since the 1950s. Before synthetic sponges existed, people used "natural sponges," which are jelly-like marine creatures that live at the bottom of the ocean.

Sea sponges in their natural habitat.

over the side. But almost immediately, he tugs on his signal line, indicating that he wants to be brought up right away. Something must be wrong. His crew hauls him up. As soon as he gets on deck and pulls his diving helmet off, he rants and raves about all the dead bodies he just saw lying at the bottom of the sea—lots of them. The rest of the crew thinks maybe he's got "the bends" (see "Diving Difficulties" box, page 45), and that his strange ramblings are a result of the nitrogen in the breathing mix that's been piped into his diving helmet. Nevertheless, the captain dives overboard to take a look. He isn't down long, either. He tugs. They haul him up. When he emerges, he's waving a human arm over his head.

The arm is made of bronze. It's a piece of a statue. Turns out, they've stumbled upon something a lot more interesting than sea sponges.

DiVING DiFFICULTiES

An old-school diving suit from the twentieth century.

In ancient times, sponge divers gathered sponges from the ocean floor with no special equipment other than a heavy, flat stone on a rope. The diver took hold of the stone, drew a deep breath, and dove to the bottom.

The stone helped him get to the bottom rapidly. Once on the ocean floor, the diver cut away as many sponges as he could, and stashed them in a net bag fastened to his waist.

Good divers could stay underwater for as long as three to five minutes.[2]

By about 1865 a new technology was invented. The diver wore a rubber suit and an astronaut-like round helmet, which was attached to an air hose that piped in compressed air from the surface and which allowed the diver to stay underwater for as long as twenty minutes. This extra time at the bottom allowed fishermen to find a lot more sponges. But early divers paid a terrible price for the increased efficiency. For decades no one understood the dangers when divers rose to the surface too quickly, without taking time to "decompress." Dissolved gases from the compressed air tube formed bubbles inside the diver's body and made him sick. This sickness was known as "the bends," and it could—and did—kill many a young man. Others were left with severe joint pain and headaches. Still others became paralyzed for life.

Modern divers now know that to avoid the bends, they must rise much more slowly to the surface.[3]

....
2   The world record for holding your breath underwater is twenty-four minutes and three seconds. It's held by—no shocker—a breath-holding diver.
3   Think of it this way: If you have a very fizzy bottle of soda, you need to open it slowly by turning the cap in small increments, so the pressure inside the bottle releases a little at a time. If you opened it all at once, the soda would spew out. Same principle.

If you look carefully, you can see the sponge diver climbing out of the water and the man in the boat operating the air pump.

HOW IT WENT DOWN

The fishermen had found an ancient shipwreck. The sponge-diving captain reported the discovery to the Greek government, and divers and archaeologists arrived at the scene. A Roman ship lay at the bottom of the ocean, about 150 feet down. The archaeologists concluded that it had sunk sometime in the middle of the first century BCE while making its way back to Rome from some of the Greek colonies that the Romans had conquered. The heavily overloaded ship was laden with Greek treasure. Like the boat of the sponge divers who discovered it, the ancient ship had likely been blown off course by high winds. It had probably been dashed against the craggy, dangerous outcroppings off the Antikythera coastline.

UP FROM THE DEPTHS

In the first exploration of the wreck, which happened soon after its discovery in 1900, divers brought a treasure trove of artifacts up from the sea bottom. They found life-size bronze statues, some in beautiful condition. There were amphorae—two-handled jugs—which were the shipping containers of the ancient world. Up came perfume jars, ornate glass bowls, coins, jewelry, and gemstones. There were several life-size horse sculptures, which had probably once pulled a life-size chariot. There were about thirty marble statues, some in fragments, some badly eroded from the ocean currents. They even found some human remains. Those

The earliest excavation team.

of one person may have been female, which led to speculation that a bride had been on board, sailing with her dowry to be married in Rome.

One other curious object was recovered. It was a battered collection of bronze pieces, which had once been some sort of mechanical device. There were gear wheels, dials, and inscriptions. That mysterious device was put on display in the local museum, but was mostly ignored for fifty years. It would turn out to be the most valuable find of all.

THE ANTIKYTHERA MECHANISM

One day, early in the 1950s, a scientist came to visit the museum to see the shipwreck artifacts. He was fascinated by the curious machine on display. What function had it performed? Who had built it? The thing resembled the inside of a windup alarm clock. But this device had been created centuries before clocks were invented.

A few years later, that scientist published an academic paper about the curious object. Others read it and were equally intrigued. Mathematicians, engineers, historians, and archaeologists came to Greece to examine the thing closely. They exchanged ideas and proposed theories about its possible uses. But because it

What was this mysterious machine?

was so smooshed and corroded after lying at the bottom of the sea for two thousand years, scientists could only guess.

And then new technologies came along. Advanced imaging tools allowed researchers to glimpse beneath the battered-up exterior, and to reconstruct how the device would have worked.

A MARVELOUS MACHINE

The original device was a complex, whirling instrument with thousands of interlocking tiny teeth on the edge of at least thirty bronze gears, all of which were enclosed in a wooden container about the size of a shoebox. If you turned one main drive handle, the gears rotated. On the faces of the front and back panel, indicator needles would spin and show the positions of the planets, the phases of the moon, and predictions, both forward and backward in time, of lunar and solar eclipses. It had inscriptions and pictures of Greek zodiac signs and Egyptian calendar days. There was also tiny script that explained (in ancient Greek) how to operate the machine and what the needles would indicate. The upshot? It was a mechanical model of the Greek universe. It could calculate the rotation of the moon's orbit to a mind-blowing degree of precision. It could tell you the current day's position of the planets, or it could be turned to a future date to show what their position would be. The thing could be *programmed*. Like a *computer*. In fact, it arguably *was* a computer.

Scientists now believe that the device was so technologically advanced, nothing even close to its level of sophistication would be invented for at least 1,500 more years.

KING SWAPPING

Several hundred years before the Golden Age of Greece, Babylonian astronomers made calculations on clay tablets and had figured out the cycle of lunar and solar eclipses and how to predict them. Astronomers and astrologers used their ability to predict eclipses in order to advise the king. Because eclipses were considered a bad omen for the ruler, the Babylonians hit upon a solution: Just before an eclipse, the reigning king would abdicate (step down) temporarily.

A substitute—usually a condemned prisoner—would be appointed the king. Then, when the eclipse occurred, all the bad omens would be directed at this temporary ruler. After the eclipse, the substitute king would be killed, and the real king would return to his throne, unharmed. Problem solved![4]

A Babylonian king (far right), who looks like he's paying close attention to his astrologer-advisors.

---

4   In one case a Sumerian king had a crown put on his gardener's head and installed the gardener on the throne as the temporary king. But then the actual king died while eating hot porridge. So the gardener got to remain king.

Who had invented this wondrous thing? Perhaps it was several people, and perhaps there had been lots of these types of mechanisms. The team of scientists noted that the form of Greek used in the written instructions was unique to a place called Syracuse, in what today is Sicily. That's where the greatest mathematician of the ancient world came from. His name was Archimedes. Could he have built it? Or at least, could his ideas have led to its invention?

BACK TO THE PRESENT

There's still more to be discovered. In 2016 some skeletal remains were pulled from the Antikythera wreckage, and scientists hope to test its DNA. They might be able to learn details about the sailors—their age, gender, and even what they looked like.

The Mediterranean was the superhighway for ancient civilizations. It was where a big chunk of the ancient world transported goods, people, and ideas. Many ancient wrecks still lie on its seafloor and they will continue to reveal more and more about the past.

Chapter Six

PROVING A POINT

THE DISCOVERY

The year is 1908. The place, a cattle ranch in eastern New Mexico. A cowboy with the splendid name of George McJunkin sets off on his horse. He is the foreman of the Crowfoot Ranch, a few miles away from the small town of Folsom.

George wants to survey the damage made by a dreadful storm that recently struck the area. After storm clouds dumped thirteen inches of rain, a raging wall of water had swept through Folsom, where it carried off homes and livestock and killed seventeen people. Then it had rushed downhill toward George's ranch and gushed into the arroyo (a dry, deep-sided pathway), further widening and deepening it.

As George approaches the arroyo, he discovers a newly created, ten-foot gully that yawns open beneath some of the barbed-wire

After a flash flood in 1908, important archaeological evidence emerged.
We think the man in the picture is George McJunkin, but we're not certain.

fence. He stares into it, and notices some white things that stick out near the bottom. They're bones. Large bones. He climbs down into the ditch and digs some of them out. Then he lugs them back to his house. Later he will return and dig out more. There are a lot of them.

George McJunkin is not any old cowboy. He is a cowboy with an observant scientific mind, and he knows that these bones are something different. First, based on his experience and book knowledge, he is sure they're very old. And second, though they seem to be the bones of a bison (also known as a buffalo), they're much bigger than any bison he's ever seen before. He is convinced they came from some extinct creature.

He writes many letters to alert people of his discovery, but no one pays attention. After all, he's just a cowboy, and a Black cowboy at that. Nearly twenty years will go by before scientists take notice of George's discovery. But what he has found, and knows to be significant, will turn out to be more dramatic and important than anything even *he* can imagine.

COWBOYS OF COLOR

Nat Love was a famous Black cowboy who lived at approximately the same time as George McJunkin.

Cowboys are a symbol of the American West, but movies and television shows have almost always depicted them as white men. That's inaccurate.

The Spanish introduced horses and cattle to North America back in the late 1400s, and during the

1500s, more and more colonists arrived with more and more horses and cattle. As large cattle ranches—known as *haciendas*—were established in Spanish Mexico in the 1700s, demand grew for young men who could rope, ride, and wrangle herds of cattle. Most of these young men were Indigenous, and they became spectacular riders. The Spanish called these early cowboys *vaqueros*. The name probably comes from the Spanish word for cow, *vaca*. By the late 1600s, vaqueros could be Indigenous, or of mixed Indian and Spanish heritage, or Black men, whose parents had been enslaved and brought to the New World by the Spanish.

The earliest American cowboys learned their skills from the vaqueros. Some American cowboys were enslaved. Even for those who were free, the work was hard, pay was low, and food was awful. After the American Civil War ended in 1865, many young Black men left the South, often from Alabama and South Carolina, and headed west toward Texas and beyond, where ranchers desperate for workers were only too happy to hire them. In the later nineteenth century, as many as one out of every four cowboys was Black.

Black and Mexican and Indigenous cowboys faced discrimination and prejudice. They received lower wages than their white counterparts. And racism has all but erased nonwhite cowboys from the history books. But recently their role in US history is finally being recognized.

THE COWBOY SCIENTIST

George McJunkin was born enslaved on a ranch in Texas in 1851. His father was a blacksmith, which is a person who makes shoes for horses, among other things. So George grew up around horses. He learned to ride and swing a lasso. Eventually his father earned enough money to buy his own freedom. He was still trying to earn enough to buy freedom for George when the American Civil War ended, and Union (Northern) soldiers arrived at the ranch to inform George and the rest of the enslaved people that they were now free.

George was a young teenager at the time. He became a skilled cattle driver, and before long ended up at the ranch in New Mexico. He loved this part of the country, where a diverse mix of Anglo, Black, Mexican, and Indigenous people coexisted among beautiful landscapes.

George McJunkin, cowboy-scientist.

George had a keen mind. He trained other cowboys to tame wild horses in exchange for reading lessons and quickly learned to read and write. He also spoke fluent Spanish. His integrity and judgment were so highly regarded by ranch owners that he was often asked to settle arguments about land boundaries. He became one of the most respected cattlemen in the country. But his real love was science. He was an avid reader of encyclopedias and science books. He collected fossils, rocks, and arrowheads. He even owned a telescope.

After his discovery of the bones, George wrote to several men whom he knew to be knowledgeable about bones and fossils. He gave them the location and description of what he called his "bone pit," but no one showed up to investigate. The arroyo where he'd found the bones was a long ride on horseback, and no one seemed eager to make the long journey. Years passed. George grew old and died in 1922.

But by then automobiles had become more affordable. The twenties were the golden age of automobile travel. More and more people owned cars, and now the bone pit that George had discovered could be reached by car. Just a few months after his death, two of the men George had written to, a blacksmith and a banker, decided to drive to the site to have a look. They were intrigued, and took a photo. In 1926 they brought the site to the attention of a scientist at the Colorado Museum of Natural History. An excavation began. Their goal was to dig up a nice ancient skeleton to mount at the museum. No one yet knew what else was about to be revealed.

Paleontologists exploring the site of George McJunkin's discovery in 1927.

THE POINT

Multiple ancient skeletons were uncovered—ultimately thirty-two, most of them intact. As George had suspected, they turned out to be the bones of giant bison that had been extinct for thousands of years.[1] But how had all those animals died together, in one place? Could human hunters have been responsible?

Some prominent scientists scoffed at this idea. At that time most scientists believed that early North Americans (sometimes

....
1 *Bison antiquus* was seven and a half feet tall and weighed 3,500 pounds. That's twice as long as a cow and as heavy as a Jeep.

called Paleo-Indians) had been on the continent since only about 2000 BCE. Humans couldn't possibly have been around in 8000 BCE, when these bison died.

And then, in 1927, excavators at the site found proof that humans *had* been around: A spear point was discovered, still embedded in the ribs of one of the bison. That was proof that a spear thrown by a human being had killed the animal, and *that* meant that humans—from this point called Folsom people, after the nearby town—had coexisted with ancient animals at least ten thousand years ago. Scientists theorized that this had

George McJunkin found the evidence to prove that humans coexisted with these ancient bison.

been a "kill site." Hunters had herded the bison into a valley with high walls, from which the animals couldn't escape, and hurled spears at them. This was a hugely significant leap in archaeological knowledge, and in our understanding of early North Americans.

After the Folsom site discovery, more newly discovered sites revealed the existence of humans alongside now-extinct animals. Some of the artifacts found were even older than those at the Folsom site.

BACK TO THE PRESENT

George McJunkin's discovery proved more than one point. Most scientists today accept the theory that the earliest people in North America arrived from Asia by walking across a frozen super-highway in an area now known as the Bering Strait. But a great many Indigenous peoples of the Americas dispute this theory. Their creation stories tell of people who arrived by boat, during periods when ocean levels were much lower and when sea crossings were shorter. Others tell of people who came from lands to the south. Discoveries such as George McJunkin's prove how much more scientists have to learn about early humans and where they came from.

Nowadays the Folsom site is one of the best-known archaeological sites in North America. It's a New Mexico State Monument. George McJunkin received no mention in articles that documented this remarkable finding at the time. Most likely they ignored his contribution because he was a Black man. The twenties and thirties were a racist time in American history. Credit for the discovery went to the two white men who visited the site after George's death. It wasn't until recently that his contribution to our understanding of early humans in the New World was given credit.

But now you know his name.

Chapter Seven

PALEO PAINTERS

THE DISCOVERY

The year is 1940. The place, a pine forest near the town of Montignac, in the southwest part of France. World War II has begun, and Germany has just invaded France. The Nazis occupy Paris and other parts of northern France, but Montignac is part of what is known as the "Free Zone."[1] Lots of war refugees have streamed into the area.

One day in early September, four teenage boys head out into the pine forest behind the manor house called Lascaux (pronounced las-KOH). They've heard a rumor that there's an underground passageway somewhere around here, and that it

....

1   Unlike the rest of France, this area is not yet occupied by the Nazi German army. Later in the war, the Nazi Germans will occupy all of France, including Montignac. France will be liberated in 1944.

might lead to the old manor house. One of them, Marcel Ravidat, has brought his dog, Robot. Marcel is training to become a garage mechanic.

The boys hear Robot bark. The dog has gotten tangled in some brambles in the roots of a tree that has blown down. They clear an opening to free the dog, and discover a hole. They're able to peer in and see that it pitches downward, into a dark, almost vertical shaft. They throw stones into it and listen for the stones to hit bottom, to determine how far down the shaft goes. They decide to return to it later, with flashlights and proper equipment.

Four days later, Marcel returns. This time he's brought along a different friend, a fifteen-year-old boy named Jacques Marsal. Also with them are two other boys, Simon Coencas, fifteen, and Georges Agniel, seventeen, who are refugees from the war.

Marcel is the first to shinny down into the dark shaft, head-first. The other boys follow him into the hole. When they raise their lamps, they realize they are standing in a large cavern, and that the walls are covered with paintings. They explore the cavern more carefully and find more passageways that lead to more chambers. All the walls are covered in beautiful, colorful artwork and carvings. There are charging bulls, galloping horses, and leaping deer. Some images are huge. Some extend high above the boys' heads. The overall effect is breathtaking.

They tell a few of their friends. After word spreads among the kids in the village, the boys decide that their discovery must be shared with a grown-up. They notify their old schoolmaster,

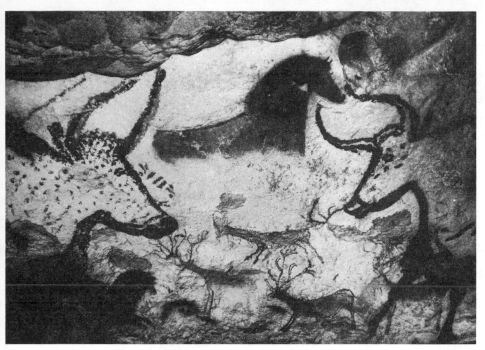

The walls of the Lascaux cave are a riot of color and motion.

Monsieur Laval. Leon Laval is a member of the local prehistory society.

With some difficulty, Monsieur Laval inches his way down into the cavern. He immediately realizes the paintings are authentically ancient, and that it is a huge discovery. "Once I arrived in the great hall accompanied by my young heroes, I uttered cries of admiration at the magnificent sight that met my eyes," he later says.

Monsieur Laval and some of the boys.

For the remainder of the war, the secrets of the cave are known only to locals.

French resistance fighters use it to store weapons to fight against the Nazi occupiers. It isn't until after the war that the rest of the world will learn about this wondrous discovery.

In 1948, after the war is over, the family that owns the estate opens the cave to visitors, who arrive by the thousands to behold the incredible prehistoric artwork. From now on, it will be known as the Lascaux cave.

A CREATIVE CULTURE

The creators of the Lascaux paintings lived during the Stone Age, which archaeologists have divided into three separate periods: Paleolithic, Mesolithic, and Neolithic. Lascaux painters lived during the Upper Paleolithic, about 17,000 to 19,000 years ago. They belonged to a culture now known as the Magdalenian. They resembled modern humans. If you saw a group of Magdalenians in dim lighting, you might not notice anything out of the ordinary, although you might wonder about the buffalo-skin clothing and the fact that they only stood about five feet tall. They lived at a time just after the Ice Age, so they enjoyed a mild climate similar to what it is in the region of France today.

The Magdalenians were hunter-gatherers, which means they lived before people knew how to plant crops for food. They hunted animals and collected wild fruits, nuts, and berries. Thanks to the mild climate, they didn't have to spend every waking moment hunting and gathering in order to put food on the table. So they were able to develop a pretty complex culture. They produced paintings, made ornaments, and created ceremonial spaces. They danced and played music. They made tools out of more sophisticated materials than mere stone or flint,[2] including bone and antler. They even used bone needles for sewing.

The Magdalenians painted images of the bison they hunted (*Bison priscus*, a species now extinct). The animals could be six and a half feet tall, with long horns. It would have been a big cause for celebration for a tribe to kill an animal the size of a minivan. One animal would have provided as much as 1,500 pounds of meat, as well as fat for lamp fuel, bones for tools and engravings, and skin for clothing, boots, and tent coverings.

CAVE WALL CANVASES

No one ever actually lived in the Lascaux cave. Scholars believe the painted chambers were used as places for spiritual rituals or for sacred ceremonies. By dating layers of sediment (see page 186), archaeologists determined that a landslide sealed off access to the cave about 13,000 BCE, which helped to both preserve it and hide it for thousands of years.

The main cavern is about sixty-six feet wide and sixteen feet high. With the other chambers and passageways off the main cavern, it extends about eight hundred feet in total. There are images of nearly six hundred animals—including wild horses, deer, bison, ibexes, big cats, reindeer, and an extinct animal called an auroch, which is an ancestor of today's ox. There are also mysterious symbols. The paintings and engravings are colored in different

....
2   Flint is a hard, rocklike form of a mineral called quartz.

Marveling at the magnificence.

shades of red, black, brown, and yellow. Some of the animals are huge (sixteen feet long), and there's even one image of a human, who seems to be a hunter. He also seems to be dead, possibly killed while hunting the large wounded animal depicted next to him.

Some archaeologists have suggested that the Lascaux cave paintings might have been created by female artists. For one thing, there are a lot of depictions of pregnant animals. For another, some handprints and a footprint found in the caves appear to be those of females. And finally, the paintings show animals in calm and reverent poses, rather than violent and aggressive ones. Perhaps while the men were out hunting, the women did a bit more than just gathering.

PRODUCING THE PAINTINGS

Making cave art required advance preparation. Artists had to create the colors,[3] make the brushes, and build scaffolding to reach the higher areas.

Artists worked in tough conditions. First, it was dark. Assistants would have held a smoky light for the artist to paint by—a stone

....
3   They made them mostly from ground-up minerals.

lamp with a well, filled with animal fat in which a flickering wick floated. Second, it must have been cold deep inside the cave for much of the year. Some of the handprints on the walls are missing fingers. That could suggest that people suffered the effects of frostbite. And third, it was awkward—artists had to climb scaffolding and paint thirteen feet above the cave floor.

They probably applied colors with brushes made of animal hair, vegetable stems, and feathers, and engraved the walls with bone tools. Some scientists believe that to produce large areas of color, artists blew paint through a tube, possibly a hollow reed, in an early version of airbrushing. Others speculate that the artists may have colored large areas with a kind of spongy ball of animal hair mixed with a vegetable fiber.

CAVEMEN? NOT

You know how people use the expression "since caveman days?" Well, there was no such thing. It's highly unlikely that our early human ancestors lived in caves. The Magdalenians were nomadic, and they probably lived in huts and tents. Most likely they came back to the same places every year, following the migrations of the animals they hunted.

⧗ BACK TO THE PRESENT

Sadly, the once perfectly preserved paintings have become damaged from too many human visitors. When the entrance was widened for visitors, the light changed and the temperature inside the cave rose.

The hundreds of thousands of tourists exhaled carbon dioxide and tracked in pollen dust, which led to an alarming growth of mold and fungi on the cave walls. The cave was closed to visitors in the 1960s. In 1983 a partial replica (copy) of the cave was opened nearby. Only a handful of scientists and special visitors are permitted to enter the real cave every year. Even so, many scientists warn that the paintings are still in grave danger of permanent damage. Let's hope modern scientists can find a way to save this spectacular window into our ancient past.

Early throngs of visitors. Nowadays the caves are closed to tourists.

Chapter Eight

THE CASE OF THE COPPER COINS

◗ THE DISCOVERY

The year is 1944. The place, a remote island in the Arafura Sea, off the northern coast of Australia. An Australian soldier named Maurie Isenberg stands on the beach. This area is full of uncharted shoals, and a notoriously dangerous place for ships. Wrecks have happened frequently over the centuries.

Maurie is a radar operator, and he's stationed on Marchinbar Island, the most northern part of the now-deserted chain known as the Wessel Islands. Australia is at war—World War II. The Australians are fighting on the side of the Allies, along with Great Britain, France, the US, and Russia. Maurie's orders are to keep an eye out for enemy ships, which in this part of the world are

Japanese. It's a lonely existence being stationed on this strip of islands where no one lives, but today Maurie has a day off, so he has decided to go fishing.

Looking down, he spots something, half-buried in the sand. He scoops up a small handful of coins. And then a few more. There are nine in all, and they're made of copper, and they look old. When he gets back to his base later, he will stash them in an empty tobacco tin and forget about them.

For more than three decades.

In 1979 Maurie Isenberg finally rediscovers the coins he'd found on that Australian beach long ago. He wonders if they're worth anything, and sends them to an expert. That expert sends them on to a world-renowned coin specialist. The upshot: Four of the coins turn out to be Dutch, from the eighteenth century. And the other five? They're much older. As in, probably from the fourteenth century. To further deepen the mystery, the older coins come from a place called Kilwa, thousands of miles away, clear across the Indian Ocean on the eastern coast of Africa. How did

The collection of curious coins.

these coins get to Australia at a time long before everyone thinks Australia was "discovered" by outsiders?

Isenberg donates the coins to a museum in Australia, and they cause an immediate buzz. Their very existence means that the history of Australia needs to be rewritten.

It's a world-rocker.

THE ORDER iN WHICH THEY WERE RECEIVED

The Indigenous people of Australia are thought to have come from Asia by water about 45,000 to 60,000 years ago, and possibly even longer ago than that. They've been there ever since. They're the oldest surviving culture on earth. There are many different indigenous cultures and groups of peoples in Australia. The Indigenous people who live near the northern part of Australia, close to the Wessel Islands, are known as the Yolngu.

Europeans began sailing the world in the late fifteenth century—that marked the beginning of a time now known as the Age of Exploration. European sailors generally arrived at the shore of a new place, planted a flag, and declared to the people who already lived there that a foreign monarch now owned their land, and more often than not, it would be renamed after that monarch. But it took Europeans a while to get to Australia. Sailing all the way to the Pacific Ocean from Europe proved challenging. You could choose one of two bad options—to sail east, all the way around the southern tip of Africa, or west, all the way around the southern tip of South America. Very few Europeans made it there early on, and of those who did, even fewer returned alive and well. So even as late as the eighteenth century, Europeans knew next to nothing about Australia.

THE EUROPEAN INVASION

In the sixteenth-century quest for global domination, Spain and Portugal were the power players. Back in 1494 the pope had actually drawn a line on the map of the world. He'd granted half the "unexplored" lands to Spain and half to Portugal, like a parent of squabbling teenagers who are forced to share a bedroom. Spanish and Portuguese conquerors sailed the world. The goals of the conquistadors were to convert the natives to Christianity and to find gold. Not necessarily in that order. They destroyed cities and stole from, enslaved, and murdered large numbers of native people.

Around 1528 some Portuguese ships sailed close enough to the coastline of Australia to draw a somewhat indistinct map that showed a big, Australia-like landmass.

Next came the Dutch—according to European history books. The first recorded landing by foreigners on Australian soil was probably in 1606. The foreigner was a Dutch navigator named Willem Janszoon. More Dutch arrived during the 1600s. They explored and mapped a fair chunk of the coast. They named this huge continent New Holland, and the island chain in the Arafura Sea the "Wesel" Islands.

Did you catch that date? This "first" landing in Australia

happened two hundred years *after* the dates of the Kilwa coins Maurie found. In Australia. Had explorers from Africa gotten there first?

New Holland didn't seem to have any gold or other promising natural resources such as "sandal-wood, nutmegs, cloves or other spices," and some of the natives proved less than thrilled about being discovered. One Dutch explorer complained that when he and his shipmates attempted to come ashore, the natives "let fly their arrows at us with great fury and loud shouts." So seventeenth-century European exploration in Australia remained lackluster.

By the 1700s Spain and Portugal had run out of steam in the power struggle for world domination. The British and the Dutch surged ahead. Great Britain's enthusiasm for boldly going where no (white) man had gone before reached something of a fever pitch.

James Cook

In 1768 King George III of England sent an explorer named Captain James Cook on Britain's first voyage of discovery to the Pacific Ocean. Cook's ship landed in southeastern Australia, and, seeing few native people (they kept their distance) and no white people, Cook declared the land to be unoccupied, and claimed it for Britain. He then proceeded to map much of the eastern coast of the continent.

MEANWHILE, BACK IN THE WESTERN HEMISPHERE

Eighteenth-century British prisons had become severely over-crowded. So Parliament hit upon a solution. British authorities put convicts on ships and sent them across the Atlantic to populate the thirteen American colonies. They called this "transporting." Because the American colonists were already steamed up about taxation and representation, the British practice of transporting criminals into their neighborhoods didn't do much to improve colonists' rebellious mood. In 1751 Benjamin Franklin wrote an essay that railed against "these Thieves and Villains introduc'd among us." But King George was the king. The American colonies were part of his realm, and he could do as he pleased. What could possibly go wrong, right?[1]

The colonists rebelled. The American Revolution was fought. America became a new country. This outcome was inconvenient for the British Parliament on a number of levels, and one of them was that the British needed a new place to dump their convicted criminals. Their solution? Newly "discovered" Australia! What could possibly go wrong, right?

In 1787 British authorities transported a group of 736 convicts to Australia. The convicts ended up at a place that would later become the city of Sydney. Transportation to Australia became more or less a regular thing. No one asked the Indigenous people how they felt about their new neighbors.

....

1 For more on what could possibly go wrong, go find a book about the American Revolution and read up on the part about "causes."

76

The settlement of Australia by the British quickly accelerated. The Europeans carried diseases with them, and the Indigenous people, who had been isolated for thousands of years from European and Asian germs, and had no resistance to the deadly viruses, died in droves. Smallpox was a huge killer.

In northern Australia, many of the Yolngu people were wiped out by diseases before the beginning of the nineteenth century.

Thirty-two years after Cook's voyage, the British navigator Matthew Flinders sailed all the way around the whole continent, proving that this vast land was, in fact, an island. The name was changed from New Holland to Australia in 1817. He also kept the name "Wesel" Islands, but spelled it "Wessel," which probably looked more British.

THE AFRICAN CONNECTION

Picture the continent of Africa. Better yet, find a map of it. The eastern side is directly across the Indian Ocean from Asia. Starting in the ninth century, and reaching a peak in the fourteenth and fifteenth centuries, a thriving shipping network flourished in East Africa. Stone mosques and palaces were built. Port towns boomed. One of the biggest was Kilwa Kisiwani, an empire built on a small tropical island with a sheltered harbor, less than two miles off the coast of what would later be called Tanzania. Ships from Kilwa carried gold from the mines of Great Zimbabwe across the ocean to India, China, and Indonesia. Others exchanged slaves, ivory, timber, and ambergris (waxy gunk from the intestines of whales, used to make perfume) for cotton from India and

Kilwa Kisiwani, in the sixteenth century.

porcelain from China. In the fifteenth century, there was even a sudden demand in China for African giraffes, which were shipped to the imperial court.

Everything changed in 1505 when the Portuguese showed up. Their ships rounded the southern tip of Africa and sailed up the east side. After their initial astonishment at finding busy ports and thriving cities, the Portuguese conquistadors did what they typically did, and proceeded to murder, terrorize, burn, and destroy everyone and everything in their path. The coastal port cities of Africa that had long traded with China, India, the Spice Islands, and Arabian Persia were looted and burned to the ground. Including Kilwa.

At the time that Maurie Isenberg's discovery came to light, no coins from Kilwa had been found anywhere else in the world, except one in Zimbabwe in Africa, and one in Oman, in the Persian Gulf. How—and when—did they get to that beach in the northern part of Australia?

But enough about coins for now. Let's talk about large, soft-bodied sea creatures that can spew their internal organs out of their butts.

GLOBULAR BLOBS

These unlovely creatures are commonly known as sea cucumbers, which is confusing because they are definitely animals and not vegetables. Indonesians call them trepangs. They're a favorite food in China, and are also used as medicine. Scientists believe there are about 1,200 different species, and possibly way more.

They may not look cute and cuddly, but sea cucumbers are rather remarkable creatures.

Sea cucumbers live fairly dull lives at the ocean bottom, where they slurp up sea junk and poop it back out again. Some species resemble giant earthworms, but others come in eye-popping colors and wacky shapes. Various species have various ways of defending themselves when threatened. Some spit out sticky string. Others do, in fact, shoot some of their internal organs out of their butts.[2] And though nowadays, many species have been overfished and are endangered, these animals were once plentiful . . . in the Arafura Sea, near the Wessel Islands.

Hold that thought.

2   But not to worry—the organs quickly regenerate!

WHAT THE YOLNGU KNEW

According to Yolngu oral history, Europeans were not the first outsiders to visit Australia. The Yolngus' ancestors had been trading with Indonesians for hundreds of years prior to the arrival of white Europeans. Specifically, they'd traded with fishermen from a part of Indonesia known as Makassar. The Makassans had discovered that the waters of the Arafura Sea near the Wessel Islands had lots of trepang. As noted (see box on page 79), there was a booming demand for trepang in China.

BACK TO THE PRESENT

Is your head spinning with all the different angles to this mystery? All these coins, colonies, convicts, Kilwa, and cucumbers? There's a concept in science that's called parsimony, and it's a principle that says to choose the simplest scientific explanation that fits the evidence you have.

So let's look at some theories as to how the Kilwa and Dutch coins got to the Wessel Islands.

1. Yolngu people were given the coins by trepang fishermen from Indonesia, as gifts in exchange for allowing them to fish there. The dates of the later coins—1780s— would support this theory, because that's when many historians believe that trepang fishermen really ramped up their fishing in the area.

Or . . .

2. Maybe a Dutch vessel was shipwrecked. Maybe the coins washed ashore and were found by the Yolngu.

Or . . .

3. Maybe Yolngu adventurers hopped onto Makassan boats and traveled to other places, including Singapore and the Philippines. Perhaps they brought back some coins. There may even have been a robust trade between the Yolngu and the Makassans. One fact that supports this theory is that there are hundreds of shared words in the language of the two cultures.

It's a mystery for sure. Ever since they came to light, the Wessel coins have been a source of fascination and speculation the world over. Lots of people have gone to the Wessel Islands looking for further clues. Recently, Indigenous Australian rock art has been found that seems to depict a foreign sailing vessel, one that far predates Cook's arrival. In 2018 an amateur archaeologist searched on a different island in the same Wessel chain. He found another ancient coin, and it's believed to be from Kilwa.

The plot thickens.

Chapter Nine

SCROLL UP

THE DISCOVERY

The year is 1947. The place, an area of the Sahara Desert near the Dead Sea. It looks like the middle of nowhere, but it's just a day's donkey ride from the cities of Jerusalem or Bethlehem, and a two-hour walk to the city of Jericho. A young goatherd named Mohammed has lost track of one of his goats near some craggy cliffs. Mohammed is a Bedouin (pronounced BED-uh-win), which is the term used to describe nomadic Arab desert dwellers. On a treeless, grassless plateau not far from an ancient ruin called Qumran, he spies the opening of a cave. Maybe his goat is in there? He chucks a stone into the dark interior. He figures that if the goat is inside, it will be startled enough to run back out again. Instead he hears something inside the cave shatter. This concerns him, because he doesn't expect such a sound.[1] He decides not to explore the cave all by himself.

Mohammed tells another boy—one of his relatives—and they return the next day to the cave. They find no goat. But they do find shards of broken pottery, and also quite a few large clay jars that are still in one piece. Inside seven of the jars are some rolled-up scrolls wrapped in dusty linen. They collect the scrolls and take them back to camp to show them to the grown-ups. Someone unrolls the scrolls. They're covered in strange writing. The boys roll them back up and stuff them into their saddlebags. They'll take them to Bethlehem on the next market day and see if they can sell them.

The curious containers inside the cave.

In Bethlehem a few days later, the boys show the scrolls to a merchant who goes by the name of Kando. Kando is the Bedouin's go-to buyer. He purchases the butter and cheese they make, as well as any interesting antiques the Bedouin find in the desert that Kando can sell to foreign tourists. Kando has no idea what these strange documents might be, but he suspects foreigners could be

....
1   You'll understand, if you've ever, say, hit a baseball a little off-kilter and then heard the sound of your neighbor's window shattering.

THE DEAD SEA

In Hebrew it's called the Salt Sea. In Arabic it's called the Sea of Death. It's really a lake, and it stretches across about sixty miles of Israel, Jordan, and the Palestinian "West Bank." It's so salty, no marine life can survive in it except some bacteria. The Jordan River flows into it. Because Syria, Lebanon, Israel, and Jordan have diverted the Jordan River's water for decades, the lake has rapidly shrunk. It's also the lowest elevation on the surface of the earth.

Because the Dead Sea is so salty, people can easily float on the surface.

interested in them. He takes them to a professor he knows. The professor contacts a few other people. Eventually Kando manages to find a buyer for four of the scrolls, for what amounts to about $300.

The news about these mysterious scrolls spreads. The first scrolls end up in the hands of several scholars, who quickly realize their importance. Are there more where these came from? Bedouin and archaeologists step up the search. They find more caves, and thousands more rolls and fragments of ancient manuscripts.

The texts will soon become known as the Dead Sea Scrolls. They're the most important religious texts ever found.

TEXT TREASURES

The scrolls are written on animal skin, parchment, and papyrus. One is even written on flattened copper. The texts vary in their lengths—one scroll is twenty-six feet long. The scrolls date back to between 200 BCE and 70 CE. They include every book of the Hebrew Bible (except the book of Esther)—it's what Christians call the Old Testament. There are also hymns, prayers, and the earliest known version of the Ten Commandments. Other scrolls describe detailed information about Jewish life from that time period. Written in ancient Hebrew, Aramaic, and Greek, the scrolls have added new perspectives on early Jewish and Christian history.

A piece of precious parchment.

WHAT A BARGAIN!

At the time the scrolls were discovered, there was great turmoil in the area. (There still is.) World War II had recently ended, and the newly formed United Nations had just created a brand-new homeland for Jewish people—Israel. The Palestinian people who already lived in the territory believed they had a rightful claim to the land. In 1948 war broke out. By the 1950s the location of the caves where the scrolls had been found had become known as the West Bank (of the river Jordan).

Amid all the wartime disruption in Jerusalem, a collector bought four scrolls from Kando, and then traveled to the US to try to find universities willing to buy them. He failed to drum up much interest. In 1954 he placed an ad in the *Wall Street Journal* in the classified section under "Miscellaneous Items for Sale" that read:

> *Biblical Manuscripts dating back to at least 200 BCE, are for sale. This would be an ideal gift to an educational or religious institution by an individual or group.*

For a religious scholar, stumbling upon an ad like this would be the equivalent of someone in search of a used car who finds an ad selling the Batmobile for next to nothing.

Eventually seven of the original scrolls were purchased by the brand-new state of Israel.

The 1948 Arab-Israeli War kept scholars from examining the area where Mohammed found the caves, near the Qumran ruins, but in 1951, with a rickety peace in place, archaeologists descended on the site to try to try to find out more information. Starting with the obvious questions: Who had made the scrolls? Why had they hidden them away in the caves? Why had they not returned for them?

WHO MADE THE SCROLLS?

The origin of the Dead Sea Scrolls is hotly debated in scholarly circles to this day. Some scholars believe they were created somewhere away from Qumran, and were written by multiple Jewish groups. Another theory is that the scrolls were produced by a Jewish sect commonly known as the Essenes. We know about

Some of the caves in the area where the scrolls were discovered.

them from the writings of a Jewish historian in ancient Rome named Josephus. The Essenes were a group of all-male Jewish monks who (may have) lived in Qumran around the first century CE, and who devoted their lives to copying and preserving religious texts. They broke from the rest of the Jewish community because the Essenes believed others were not devout enough. The Essenes were *quite* devout. They did not marry or own any property. They had strict procedures for praying, fasting, and observing the Sabbath—including a rule that they were not supposed to poop on the Sabbath. It's unclear how that rule worked.

But there are scholars who believe Josephus made all that stuff up. No one is entirely certain who actually lived in Qumran. It may have been a fort built by Jews to protect themselves. It may have been just a pottery factory or a tannery.

WHO PUT THE SCROLL iN THE CAVES?

The Romans conquered the area in 63 BCE. About a hundred and thirty years later, Jewish people in Jerusalem rose up in protest. They tried—and failed—to gain political and religious independence from Rome. After a siege of the city in 68 CE, Roman soldiers bashed their way in and destroyed the Jewish temple, along with much of the city. They slaughtered most of the inhabitants and enslaved the rest.

What happened next is also hotly debated by scholars. Those who don't buy the Essenes theory think that Jews living in Jerusalem saw in advance that their sacred texts were in peril and gathered everything they could from libraries and other collections. They fled the city—possibly escaping by way of the sewers—and then hurriedly stuffed the scrolls in the Qumran caves to hide them from the advancing Roman army. Why the people who hid them didn't return for them remains a mystery.

BACK TO THE PRESENT

In 2017 a new cave was discovered that contained broken urns that once held Dead Sea Scrolls. This recent find has excited scholars. Many now believe there may be more scrolls hidden in the hundreds of additional caves in the area.

So there may be much left to discover and uncover. And it's all thanks to a wayward goat.

Chapter Ten

BOGGED DOWN

THE DISCOVERY

The year is 1950. The place, Central Jutland, an area in the middle of the country of Denmark. Eleven-year-old John Kausland digs peat with his mother, stepfather, and step-uncle. John's family lives in the nearby village of Tollund, a few miles from this peat bog.

Suddenly John's mother, Grethe Højgaard, stops digging. She stares down into the peat. "There's something strange here," she announces.

Now there's an understatement.

The others crowd around Grethe to look.

They see a body half-submerged in the soggy peat. It's the body of a man. But this is not an old Celtic legend, and it's not a horror movie. The dead guy does not stand up and stride out of the fen, looking like a googly-eyed glob of creamed spinach.

MAGICAL MYSTERY MARSH

••

Bogs are common in this flat, marshy part of
Denmark. Bogs form in water-soaked, low-lying areas
where decaying plant matter builds up. Over centuries,
layers of dead plant material heap up in the bog, and one
type of plant material in particular is known as sphagnum
moss. Eventually the organic matter turns into brown
spongy gunk called peat. For ages, peat has been cut and
dried and used as fuel to heat homes.

Besides being sources of peat, bogs have always been

Bogs: a ghostly gateway to the next world?

considered magical, ghostly places by local people. Celtic legends depict them as portals between the world of the living and the world of the dead. And you can't really blame people for thinking this, because sometimes at dusk, bogs give off an eerie green glow. Sometimes at night, balls of blue light hover and blink above their murky damp waters. (Thank you, bioluminescent marsh gases!) Bright-colored flowers called asphodels light up the bog like stars. Or fairy crowns. Nearly every country in northwestern Europe where bogs are found has myths and legends about bogs.

No, the man Gerthe has uncovered looks like . . . us. His face is so calm and fresh he appears to be asleep. But he is most certainly not asleep—he's dead. More alarming still, everyone can clearly see that there's a rope cinched around his neck. He died . . . violently.

The body seems to have been dumped in the bog recently, because there is no sign of decomposition. John's family calls the police to report a murder. But when the police learn that the body

Hollywood has made many horror movies featuring creepy creatures from swamps.

has been found in a bog, they call in the archaeologists.

And now we skip to nearly two years later. A team of workers is cutting peat not far from Tollund, this time near a village called Grauballe. The shovel of a peat digger whose name is Tage Busk Sørensen suddenly encounters something . . . un-peatlike. It's another dead body. Tage alerts his boss.

Because they remember the news reports about the discovery of the body in the bog at Tollund, the peat diggers don't notify the police. They notify the archaeologists.

Two days later, the body, which will later be called Grauballe Man, is transported in a big box, surrounded by the peat layers in which it had been resting, to the local museum of prehistory.

The body is put on display on the ground floor of the museum, and members of the public throng to line up to see it before it goes back to the science lab. Twenty days after the discovery, museum archaeologists are able to examine the body more closely. They discover that the throat has been slashed from ear to ear.

Turns out, bodies have been fished out of bogs around here for a long time. Not all are as well preserved as Tollund Man and Grauballe Man. (Most of the bodies are named after the towns near where they were discovered.) Many of them show signs of a violent death. Some have been strangled, others stabbed, some

He looks like he's sleeping . . . except for the rope around his neck.

92

drowned. To deepen the mystery, despite the violent and gruesome ways they'd been killed, some of the bodies look as though they had been gently placed into the bog. Whoever bludgeoned, stabbed, and strangled them didn't seem to be, well, *mad* at them.

So who killed them? How did they end up in the bogs?

SWAMP THINGS

Today they're known as "bog bodies." Over the past two hundred years, as many as one thousand bog bodies were discovered in peat bogs throughout northwest Europe—at least half of them in Denmark.

Most of the bodies found in the bogs are the remains of people who died about two thousand years ago. Many look pretty good for their age. It's slightly unsettling to be able to stare into the face of a person who's been dead for two thousand years, and to notice their glossy, braided hair, the whisker stubble on their cheeks, the pores on their nose. Tollund Man, who died in approximately 375 BCE, wore a pointy cap made of eight pieces of leather sewn together and tied under his chin.

The dead include young and old, men and women, kings and commoners. The oldest of the bog bodies that still includes skin and flesh was discovered by peat cutters in Ireland in 2011. Named Cashel Man, his body dates back four thousand years to the Bronze Age. To give you an idea of how long ago that was, at the time of Cashel Man's death, King Tut was still over six hundred years in the future.

Some bog bodies still have internal organs inside them, including the stomach, and scientists have been able to analyze the contents to determine what they had for their last meal. Both Tollund Man and Grauballe Man had eaten a gloppy gruel made from barley, linseed, and a bunch of other weeds. It contained no spring or summer vegetables, so both likely died in winter or early spring. The gruel must have tasted disgusting, but was probably reasonably nutritious. Grauballe Man had rheumatoid arthritis and swollen gums. He probably suffered from agonizing toothaches.

BOG SCIENCE

The bottom of a bog is a cold, acidic, airless place. Organic stuff breaks down super slowly. Bog water contains chemicals that can preserve bodies. Bog bodies often have dark brown, leathery skin, like a well-worn baseball glove. Their hair tends to be red—sometimes bright red—but that's most likely caused by a chemical in the moss that tints the hair after death. The sphagnum also dissolves bones. That's why so many bog bodies have no skeletons. They're just floppy, leathery bags of skin and pickled organs.

WiLD WARRiORS

Most of the people whose bodies went into the bogs lived during a period known as the Iron Age, which began about 500 BCE. The people who lived in Jutland were a Germanic tribe called the Cimbri (pronounced SIM-brey).

Classical writers describe the Cimbri as tall, blond, and blue-eyed, and that is borne out by the bog bodies found—one, called Old Croghan Man, may have been six feet, six inches tall.

Ancient Greek and Roman writers had a grudging respect for the Cimbri, who were known for their ferocious fighting. Sometimes the Cimbri went into battle naked except for a short skin cape pinned with a brooch at the shoulders. According to the Roman historian Tacitus, Germanic warriors arranged their hair by "twisting their hair and pulling it up in a knot." Tacitus suggested that their big hair made them look fiercer: "all this elaborate make-up is to impress the foe they will meet in battle." It was an effective and alarming costume.

One of the major battles between the Romans and the northern tribes happened about 125 BCE—a century or so after Tollund Man's death. The Greek historian Plutarch wrote about the Cimbri as they crossed the Alps on their way toward Rome. "They endured the snow-storms without any clothing, made their way through ice and deep snow to the summits." Then they tobogganed down the snow slopes on their shields, while emitting earsplitting yells.[1]

....
1 (Naked.)

GiVEN TO THE GODS

Northern tribes chucked a lot of stuff into bogs—shoes, weapons, slaughtered animals, and, for about five hundred years, humans. Archaeologists have even found a large container of butter. In a bog in the northern part of Jutland, a huge silver cauldron was found. It dates to about 200 BCE, and it depicts scenes of human sacrifice, including one scene where a person is either being drowned in a vat or has had his throat cut and is having his blood collected. Some historians speculate that these offerings were placed in the bog to appease the gods.

So how did they decide whom to sacrifice? What can the bog bodies tell us about themselves?

Some of the people from the bog appear to have been peasants. Their stomach contents reveal that they ate lots of plants and grains, and not much meat. Archaeologists can tell from ridges on

We're not sure what's happening to the upside-down guy
(second from left) but whatever it is, it's not good.

people's teeth that they lived through periods when there was little of anything to eat.

Others appear to have been from a higher social station, and ate a lot of meat—the diet of a wealthier person. Two female bog bodies wore good-quality clothing that had been made outside of Denmark. Does that mean they were wealthy foreigners? Or simply wealthy enough to be able to afford clothing made somewhere else?

The Gundestrupkarret cauldron. Say that five times fast!

Clonycavan Man had traces of fancy hair gel that had been imported from elsewhere—it had been made from a vegetable plant oil mixed with resin from a pine tree. His hair was tied in a Cimbric man bun on top of his head. (He was only five feet, two inches, so he might have hoped his bun made him look taller.) He also had well-manicured nails and no calluses on his hands, suggesting he did not perform manual labor. That, plus his imported hair gel and high-protein diet, indicated he had high social status.

Some historians speculate that high-born prisoners from foreign tribes (such as the two women) were chosen as sacrifices because they were foreigners. Other historians suggest that some were chieftains who were killed during bad crop years. They'd failed in their promise to the villagers to persuade the gods to deliver a successful harvest. Another interesting theory is that some were priests who lost a lottery. The sacrificed person may have drawn the short straw in a grim game of Iron Age roulette and willingly gone to his death to appease the gods that were worshipped by the people in his tribe.

BACK TO THE PRESENT

The bodies from the bog have raised a lot of questions. Who were they? Why them? Did they willingly accept their fates? Because they're so unsettlingly real-looking, they bring us face-to-face—quite literally—with the past. It's impossible not to wonder about them, even to be slightly haunted by them. They continue to fascinate archaeologists, historians, and poets to this day. We may someday learn more of the secrets the bog bodies have taken to their dark and watery graves.

Chapter Eleven

LUCKY BREAK

THE DISCOVERY

The year is 1955. The place, the city of Bangkok, Thailand. A group of monks and workmen struggles to move a giant plaster statue of the Buddha. It's nine feet tall and immensely heavy. They've been at it all day.

For twenty years the statue has sat under a tin-roofed shelter on the grounds of a temple known as the Wat Traimit (*wat* is the Thai word for a Buddhist temple). Finally it's time to move it to its new location inside the renovated temple. The men have slowly inched it along on round logs from its place in the shelter to the lawn in front of the temple. With loops of ropes, pulleys, and hooks, they strain to hoist the statue onto a platform, but they barely manage to get it a couple of inches off the ground.

Suddenly one of the ropes breaks. The Buddha bangs heavily

against the ground, and some of the plaster breaks off. Underneath is a layer of black lacquer, a shiny, nail polish–like paint.

The clouds open, and thunder and lightning put a stop to the day's work.

The next morning the monks and workers return to try again. Someone makes an effort to clear away some of the chipped black lacquer.

And then everyone stares in disbelief. Underneath the black paint, something shiny and yellow gleams.

Beneath all that painted plaster and lacquer, this statue of the Buddha is pure gold.

The gleaming Buddha as it now appears, after
all the plaster and lacquer was removed.

A BiT ABOUT THE BUDDHA

Siddhartha Gautama was a philosopher, religious teacher, and the founder of Buddhism. He was born sometime between the sixth and fourth century BCE to a royal family in northern India (today part of southern Nepal). He spent his youth in luxury, protected from the world outside his lavish palace. But when he was twenty-nine, he left the palace. Out in the world, he encountered old age, sickness, and death. He set out to discover the meaning of life and human suffering. To find that meaning, he practiced a very strict form of self-denial, but after six years, he adopted a more balanced existence (he called that path the Middle Way). At age thirty-five, while meditating under a tree, he had a spiritual breakthrough (which Buddhists now call enlightenment). From then on, he became known as Buddha, and he spent the rest of his life spreading his teachings.

Today the Buddha's life and teachings serve as the foundation of Buddhism. The name Buddha in ancient Sanskrit means "enlightened one" or "the awakened."

Nowadays Buddhist monks take vows to live according to the teachings of the Buddha. They refrain from killing, stealing, lying, and having romantic attachments. There are about 400 million Buddhists in the world. In Thailand, over 90 percent of the population is Buddhist.

Buddhist monks may not work to earn their livings. They do not eat after the sun has passed its high point (generally around noon). They are supported by regular people and by the government. There are over thirty thousand Buddhist monasteries

THE KEY TO IT ALL

As restorers carefully removed the plaster that coated the Golden Buddha, they discovered that there was a key embedded in the base of the statue. It could be used to unlock nine separate parts of the statue, which enabled it to be taken apart and cleaned and moved much more easily. This proved to be a useful function, given that the statue weighs five and a half tons—that's roughly as heavy as a full-grown elephant.

throughout Thailand. People offer wandering monks combinations of food, clothing, medicine, and shelter. Providing these "alms" allows the giver to have an improved chance for a good rebirth in their next life. In turn, monks dedicate themselves to aiding others on their paths toward enlightenment.

THIS BUDDHA'S PATH

So let's track the statue's journey through the centuries of warfare and relocation.

It's helpful to know some Thai history. Most people living in modern-day Thailand are descended from a much larger group of people who spoke a language called Tai, and who settled in the area about a thousand years ago. If you look at the map (next page), you can see that modern Thailand is in the middle of a

The country of Thailand with its modern-day borders.

peninsula and is surrounded by other countries—there's Laos to the north and east. There's Burma (today also called Myanmar) to the west. Cambodia lies to the southeast, and due north, beyond Laos, is China. Over the centuries, various kingdoms in this area rose and fell and were conquered by outside armies.

TAI, THAI, THAILAND

Tai can mean both a cultural identity and a language. Historically, Tai peoples included several culturally related groups from mainland Southeast Asia. The Tai family of languages was spoken by these different groups, including Thai (Siamese), Lao, and Shan. Today there are millions of cultural descendants of Tai peoples. Most live in Thailand, Laos, Myanmar, China, and Vietnam.

A SUKHOTHAI STATUE

We're not exactly sure when the Golden Buddha was created. But there's evidence to suggest that the statue dates back to the thirteenth century.

In 1238 two Tai princes defeated the Khmer army (from what is now Cambodia) at a place called Sukhothai. Sukhothai became the capital of the new Tai kingdom.

From 1279 to 1298(ish), a ruler named Ramkhamheng (Rama the Bold) reigned over the kingdom of Sukhothai. He ranks as one of the greatest Tai rulers, and gets credit for creating the first Thai alphabet. He also firmly established Buddhism throughout his kingdom. And then there's this intriguing clue: In 1292 some engraved stone tablets created during his reign tell of the creation of some Buddha statues, and they're described as "great" and "beautiful," and in one case, "18 cubits high." That's twenty-seven feet tall. Could that be an exaggerated description of "our" Buddha?

During his reign, Rama the Bold visited the Mongol court of Kublai Khan in China. At the time, the Mongol Empire was the most powerful kingdom in the world (see page 174). While there, Rama the Bold promised the great Khan that the Tais would pay tribute to the Mongols. This was a smart move, because it prevented the Mongols from invading Sukhothai and protected the Tai kingdom's independence. He also brought some Chinese artists back to Sukhothai. Their expertise helped pull the Tais out of the feudal era and began an era in which beautiful artwork and pottery were created. This is generally considered Thailand's

Rama the Bold.

golden age of art. The statues produced during this time are considered among the most beautiful representations of the Buddha.

THE GOLDEN STATUE'S STYLE

Of the many thousands of statues of the Buddha, most show the Buddha in one of four positions—sitting, standing, walking, or reclining.[1] All the poses, postures, and hand gestures symbolize something. The Golden Buddha sits in classic "Sukhothai Style": cross-legged with the left hand on his lap and the right hand touching the ground. That's what's known as the "earth touching posture." The flame at the top of his head is a symbol of his spirituality. He has an oval-shaped face, curved eyebrows, and a faint smile on its lips. His hair is arranged in short, twisted whorls. It's meant to symbolize the hair of the original Buddha, who cut off his princely topknot to show that he had cast off his privileged past.

THE STATUE IS MOVED TO AYUTTHAYA

The Sukhothai kingdom was independent for about two hundred years. But in 1350 a new Tai capital was established at Ayutthaya (pronounced ah-YOOT-tah-yah). For the next four hundred years, this kingdom would be the dominant power in what is now central Thailand. Many Europeans and neighboring countries

....

1   You may have seen another common figure, a jolly, laughing bald guy with a round belly. He isn't the Buddha. He's a wandering Chinese monk from the sixth century. You're supposed to rub his belly to receive good luck and fortune.

called the country Siam, so the Tai people of Ayutthaya came to be known as the Siamese.

By 1438 the once-powerful kingdom of Sukhothai had become a province of Ayutthaya. Historians think that sometime in the fifteenth century, the Golden Buddha was moved from Sukhothai to the new kingdom of Ayutthaya.

A series of all-powerful kings ruled Ayutthaya during this period. More than 100,000 people may have lived in the city at its height, which at the time meant it had more people than did London or Paris. Commoners were not allowed to look the king in the eye, and whoever addressed the king directly had to refer to themself as "the dust beneath your majesty's feet." Subjects who violated court rules were severely punished. For instance, if you kicked the palace door, you'd lose your foot. If you struck the king's elephant, you lost a hand. The penalty for whispering while in the presence of the king, or for "introducing love poems in the palace," was death. If the condemned person had noble blood, he was tied in a velvet sack and beaten with a sandalwood club.[2]

THE COVER-UP

Over the next 250 years there were near-constant battles between the Siamese and the Burmese for control of Ayutthaya. It was probably during this time of ongoing strife that someone— monks, most likely—sent the Golden Buddha into hiding. The statue was first covered in black lacquer, and then with about an

....
2   Because you weren't supposed to spill royal blood.

inch of plaster. The idea was to thwart Burmese invaders from seeing the statue's true value. The disguise obviously worked.

Between 1765 and 1767 the Siamese and the Burmese fought yet another war. An army of 1.5 million Burmese soldiers and six thousand elephants entered Ayutthaya. The city was sacked and burned to the ground. Burmese soldiers destroyed most of the artwork throughout the city, and melted down and carried away anything made of gold.

It's kind of a miracle that the statue was left whole during the Burmese sack of the city. Many other Buddha statues were toppled, smashed, or had their heads bashed off. Tens of thousands of prisoners were taken back to Burma. Temples, literary works, and Buddha icons were destroyed. One of the most beautiful cities in the world was reduced to ashes.

Soon after sacking the Siamese capital, the Burmese withdrew from the ruined city. They had to hurry home to fend off Chinese invasions on their other border. In 1767, after the Burmese had retreated from Siam, a military leader named Taksin rose to power. Within ten years he had reunified the Siamese kingdom and expanded its territory. He moved the capital close to present-day Bangkok. But he was not as good a leader as he was a soldier. Within a few years he showed signs of serious mental issues. Concerned courtiers had him overthrown in 1782. According to most sources, he was put to death (by being tied in a velvet sack and beaten with a sandalwood club). Nonetheless, Taksin is remembered today as a savior of the Thais and a symbol of resistance against the Burmese.

Rama I, the new king of Siam, established Bangkok as the

capital in 1782. The city grew and grew, until by the mid-nineteenth century it had a population of about 400,000 people.[3]

THE STATUE IS MOVED TO BANGKOK

The still-plastered-over Golden Buddha statue was probably brought to Bangkok during the reign of Rama III (1824–1851). He decreed that everything that could still be salvaged from the ruins of Ayutthaya should be transferred south to Bangkok, and the statue was probably moved then. Did anyone wonder why the "plaster" statue was so heavy? Maybe the workers tasked with moving the thing didn't dare complain.

The still-plastered-over Golden Buddha spent the nineteenth century in two different temples, and was largely ignored.

BACK TO THE PRESENT

In about 1935, the statue was moved to the Wat Traimit temple (its final location). It sat under the metal-roofed shack on the property of the monastery for twenty years. Finally, officials made plans to renovate the temple, and construction began for a new space for the statue in 1954.

In 1955 renovation of the monastery was complete. That's when the Golden Statue's secret was revealed.

Today the temple of Wat Traimit is a major tourist attraction.

....

3   Throughout its history, Thailand has successfully resisted being colonized by outside powers. And not for outsiders' want of trying.

Chapter Twelve

ETERNALLY YOURS

THE DISCOVERY

It's the spring of 1974. The place, a drought-stricken part of north-west China called Shaanxi province. Six brothers and their neighbor, all farmers who tend persimmon and pomegranate orchards, meet to decide where to dig a well. The Yang brothers' names are Zhifa, Wenhai, Yanxin, Quanyi, Peiyan, and Xinman. Their neighbor is Wang Puzhi. The Yangs' orchards extend from the foot of Mount Li.

The next morning they start to dig. After two days they begin to uncover bricks and small bits of pottery. Have they unearthed an ancient kiln?

Next they uncover a life-size terra-cotta (fired clay) body, and then a terra-cotta head.

When they're fifteen feet down, they start to find bronze arrowheads and crossbow triggers. Now it's getting weird.

This isn't the first time local people in the area have found stuff like this, but their finds rarely reach the ears of authorities. Local people are superstitious about disturbing things that have been buried. Buried things belong to the land of the dead. It's considered bad luck to find them. But the Yang brothers are determined to finish their well. Yet they find more and more artifacts that are harder and harder to ignore.

A few weeks into their well-digging, they finally contact a man named Zhao Kanmin, who runs a small county museum nearby. He rides his bicycle to the Yangs' field. Immediately he recognizes the bricks as Qin (sometimes spelled Ch'in)—meaning they were made during the Qin Dynasty, which ruled China for a brief time, from 221 to 206 BCE. Could they have found the fabled

Long columns of warriors stand in formation, ready to defend the emperor in the afterlife.

site of the two-thousand-year-old tomb of the first emperor of China, known as Qin Shi Huang Di?

Zhao convinces the Yang brothers to abandon their digging. He reports the finding to his boss, and word reaches government authorities in Beijing. Archaeologists are quickly sent to the site.

The farmers have unearthed one of the greatest archaeological finds of all time.

THE RiSE OF THE FiRST EMPERoR

Let's back up a couple thousand years, to well before the third century BCE. Back then, China was not yet a unified empire. It was a chaos of feuding states, ruled by local overlords who were constantly at war with one another.

Eventually the Qin overpowered most of the others, and in 250 BCE Prince Zichu became king of the Qin. His son Zheng, the future first emperor, was nine years old.

Zichu ruled for just four years. He died when Zheng was only thirteen, and Zheng was crowned king, overseen by a "regent," which is a minister who helps a child-king rule until he is of age. By 239 BCE, when Zheng was about twenty, he suppressed an armed uprising and punted his regent, and became the sole ruler. And then, over the course of a mere nine years (230–221 BCE), he managed to conquer all of his rivals. In 221 BCE he crowned himself emperor Qin Shi Huang Di.

The upside of his short rule was that he unified China. He centralized the government. He standardized laws, and currency, and weights and measures, and handwriting, and also axle lengths

The First Emperor, Qin Shi Huang Di.

(that all-important distance between wheels so that horse-drawn carts could travel more easily along roads across the kingdom). And speaking of roads—he built lots of them. Also walls. In 215 BCE the emperor put his general, Meng Ti'en, in charge of building the Great Wall. At the time, there were many smaller walls, but Meng repaired and connected them and built one long wall, to keep warring tribes out and the First Emperor's subjects in.

But the downside was that to do all this unifying, the First Emperor used an iron hand. He enthusiastically admired a philosophy called legalism, which was based on the idea that rulers should use strict laws and impose harsh punishments to control a population. As a result, he executed anyone who threatened his power and mercilessly exploited the peasants through taxation and overwork. Every male between fifteen and sixty was called up to help with all the building projects, and working conditions were wretched. Untended crops withered in the fields, and starvation set in. As many as a million people may have died during the seven-year construction of the Great Wall.

The First Emperor moved all the ruling families close by so he could keep an eye on them. He became obsessed with power, and increasingly unhinged. Anyone who failed to obey his smallest command would be chopped in two at the waist. He ordered all books that didn't flatter the Qin Dynasty to be burned.[1] He rounded up as many as 460 learned scholars and had them buried alive. When his eldest son, the crown prince Fusu, raised an objection, the First Emperor banished him to the northern frontier, which was not a fun place.

DEATH DEFYING

Early in his reign the emperor began planning for the afterlife—his—and started work on one of the most ambitious monuments ever: his own tomb. The building of it would last for at least thirty years. The idea was to reproduce his life on earth in a permanent form for his life in the next world.

Because an emperor needed an army in the afterlife, the First

....
1   He wanted the history of China to begin with him. So he tried to get rid of all the books about the history of China.

Emperor commissioned one made from terra-cotta, which included thousands of soldiers ready to serve him. Life-size action figures! He also ordered terra-cotta horses, chariots, acrobats, musicians, and birds for his water garden. The army figures were all dressed according to status, in terra-cotta armor that was painted to look like the original leather. There were generals, officers, foot soldiers, cavalrymen, archers, and charioteers. No two faces were alike. Each had a unique, sometimes elaborate hairstyle, as well as beards, mustaches, and headgear. The clay was sealed with lacquer, painted in bright colors made from ground minerals, and then fired in kilns. The soldiers held real weapons—crossbows, spears, and arrows.

A terra-cotta warrior with an awesome man bun. Different hairstyles indicate the soldier's rank.

The number of laborers, builders, craftsmen, artisans, metalsmiths, and engineers required to put this massive tomb together boggles the mind. Pits were dug, wooden beams cut, and work on the standing figures conducted at breakneck speed. The bodies were molded from a few standard body types, and then customized with heads, hats, shoes, hairstyles, and beards, in a kind of ancient Chinese version of Mr. Potato Head. Once constructed, the eternal army was put into storage while the emperor lived and reigned.

ASSASSINATION ATTEMPTS

For someone who made such elaborate plans for the afterlife, it may seem strange that the First Emperor was also increasingly obsessed with finding a way to live forever. It's possible three failed assassination attempts on him had something to do with that. The first time, early in his reign, the attacker tried (but failed) to stab the emperor with a poison dagger. The second time, a blind lute player tried to bash him over the head with his lead-filled lute and missed. The third time, a would-be assassin ambushed the wrong carriage. (The emperor often traveled with duplicate imperial-looking carriages for just that reason.) The emperor took daily potions that he believed would prolong his life.

ROYALLY PARANOID

The emperor ordered all the roads connecting his 270 palaces to be walled and roofed so that he could travel from one to another without anyone knowing where he was.

One day a meteorite fell to earth. Someone engraved it with a dire message: "The First Emperor will die and his land will be divided." Furious, he ordered an investigation. When no one confessed to creating the message, he had all the local people executed and the meteorite destroyed. But the prediction was correct. It was, in fact, the last year of his life.

Not long after the meteorite incident, the emperor's counselors suggested he take a tour of his dominions. He set out with his entourage of close advisors and servants. Also with him was his eighteenth son, Huhai.

While he was far from the capital, the emperor took ill suddenly—no one knows with what—and died. So much for all those immortality potions. Fearing an uprising, and plotting their own power grab, his two closest advisors kept the emperor's death secret. The procession made its way back to the capital, with the coffin containing the dead emperor hidden away inside a closed carriage. But they were many days' journey from home, it was summer, and it was hot, so the body soon began to smell. To disguise the stench, the advisors ordered several carts loaded with stinky salted fish to join the procession back to the capital.

Something about the imperial procession smelled fishy.

When they arrived at last, fifty days later, the advisors announced the emperor's death and declared that the young and easily controlled Huhai, son number eighteen, would become the second emperor.

Then came the scramble to get the tomb ready. The eight thousand or so warriors, chariots, bronze water birds, and other assorted figures were taken out of storage and lined up in huge pits, facing east, poised to battle the First Emperor's former enemies.

The First Emperor was buried separately in his own tomb deep inside a mountain of packed earth. According to one historian who was writing about a hundred years later and so was not around personally to confirm, automatic crossbows were rigged up so they'd shoot down any looters who tried to enter the tomb, and rivers of liquid mercury were created to flow and circulate mechanically around the tomb. Mercury, a metallic element that is liquid at room temperature, is quite poisonous.

AFTER HiS DEATH

There followed four years of chaos and rebellion. At some point roaming bands of soldiers broke into one of the warrior pits and stole many of the weapons, and then set fire to a good bit of it. The weak Second Emperor was quickly overthrown, and the very short-lived Qin Dynasty ended. It was succeeded by the long-lived Han Dynasty (206 BCE–220 CE). Grass and trees grew over the emperor's tomb, and it was forgotten for over two thousand years.

Today the First Emperor's tomb remains unopened, its contents unknown. In fact, a relatively small percentage of the terra-cotta warriors has been excavated, because as soon as they're released from their earthy pit, a kind of mold starts to grow on the clay, especially when it's exposed to damp air, and the figures decay quickly.

Recently scientists have figured out how to stave off the decay. They whisk the warrior away to a climate-controlled area and apply a kind of fixative to the lacquer to keep the paint from peeling away. But excavations continue to proceed slowly and cautiously.

As for the emperor's actual burial chamber—who's to know if there are automatic crossbows ready to shoot down intruders? More concerning is the possibility that rivers of mercury might actually be down there. If so, it could be dangerous when archaeologists ultimately do gain entry.

Since the initial discovery by the Yang brothers, some six hundred pits across a twenty-two-square-mile area have been identified. Some may stay buried. Some may be excavated. It's going to take much more time to find, catalog, and analyze what's still buried there.

Chapter Thirteen

TEMPLE OF GLOOM

THE DISCOVERY

The year is 1978. The place, a busy street corner in the heart of bustling Mexico City. A group of utility workers is laying electric cable.

One of the men digging deep below street level strikes something hard with his shovel. It's a stone. But not just any stone. This one appears to be a large, flat-topped, circular stone. He can see that it's decorated with mysterious carvings.

The utility work stops. This is Mexico City. Everyone knows there's a

The carved stone discovered by the construction worker.

lot of history here. Many centuries ago, before it was Mexico City, it was called Tenochtitlán (pronounced te-nawch-tee-tlahn) and was home to a civilization most people now call the Aztec. (They called themselves the Mexica, meh-SHI-ka, or the Tenocha.)

The utility company notifies the Mexican Institute of Anthropology and History. Two days later archaeologists arrive at the scene. They begin to excavate the stone.

It's huge—ten feet across. Historians identify the figure on the stone as the Aztec Moon Goddess called Coyolxauhqui (pronounced koh-yohl-SHAW-kee).

With growing excitement, archaeologists realize that the stone lies at the base of the ruins of an Aztec temple. And not just any temple. It was once the largest and most sacred Aztec temple of all. Today it's known as the Templo Mayor.

WHO WERE THE AZTEC?

Around the year 1000 CE, early ancestors of the Aztec came down from the north (possibly from what is the southwest part of the US today) and settled in the Valley of Mexico. Around 1325 they were chased by enemy warriors to the marshes of Lake Texcoco. On an island in the middle of that lake, they founded the city of Tenochtitlán.

One of the first orders of business was to build a temple to their supreme god. The god's name was Huitzilopochtli (pronounced wee-tsee-loh-POHCH-tlee) and he was the god of the sun and also the god of war. As the city grew, the Templo Mayor was enlarged and reconstructed at least seven times. By the 1400s

121

The Templo Mayor (left center) at the heart of the Aztec Empire,
as depicted by a modern-day artist.

it had become an enormous stone pyramid as tall as a thirty-story building.

The Aztec worshipped a number of gods and goddesses. Nearly every profession prayed to at least one god. There was a goddess of salt makers, and a god of mats and basket weavers. Florists had a goddess. Feather workers who decorated warriors' helmets and shields had their own god. There were at least four gods of corn.

Some of the major Aztec gods—notably Huitzilopochtli—had extremely bad tempers. The Aztec believed that these angry gods expected to be nourished with a steady stream of human blood, and that if the gods didn't receive it, the sun would not rise in the morning and the rains would dry up and the crops would not grow. In short, the world would end. To satisfy these gods the Aztec practiced human sacrifice. That's when you kill people—usually in highly unpleasant ways—in the name of a god. (See pages 125–126.) And most of these killings occurred at the top of the Templo Mayor.

DAILY LiFE

Below the emperor were the warriors and priests. Boys from noble families who wanted to become elite warriors began training around the age of ten. Other nobly born boys (and some girls) trained to be priests at a cheery-sounding school known as the

Some members of Aztec nobility, sporting fine fashions.

Calmécac (pronounced kahl-MAY-kahk, it literally means "house of tears").

Although always at the ready to be called to battle, most ordinary Aztec men worked as farmers, fishermen, weavers, and builders. Farmers paddled their canoes through the canals that crisscrossed the city, and tended their maize fields across the lake. They grew vegetables on floating gardens made of mud and reeds. At the city's enormous marketplace, people traded for foods, textiles, and all sorts of luxury items, including jade, leopard skins, and exotic bird feathers.

Men mostly wore loincloths, colorful cloaks, and sandals. Women wore ankle-length skirts and cotton blouses. Sometimes, to be *extra* fashion-forward, Aztec women painted their teeth black or scarlet.

PLAY BALL

A favorite game of the Aztec required a great deal of skill and stamina. The goal was to be the first to get a rubber ball through a small hole in a stone ring twenty feet off the ground. The catch was, you could only touch the ball with your hips, elbows, and knees. Players on the losing team were often sacrificed.

THE EMPiRE EXPANDS

The Aztec kingdom, and Tenochtitlán especially, grew rapidly during the reign of the emperor Moctezuma the First (1440–1469). Eventually the Aztec would rule an empire of millions of people. At its height, the city of Tenochtitlán may have had as many as 200,000 inhabitants. That was larger than every other European city at the time except Constantinople.

Here's how Tenochtitlán grew so powerful: The Aztec emperor sent ambassadors to neighboring cities and tribes to demand that they pay a "tribute" to Tenochtitlán—gold, silver, cloth, whatever product that city produced. If the neighboring city refused to pony up, Tenochtitlán declared war, and an army of thousands of warriors marched in and looted it.

Aztec warriors were fearsome fighters. They fought with swords, darts, bows and arrows, and axes, all made of animal bones and sharp-edged stone. Slings and seven-foot-long spears were disturbingly effective. To make bad matters worse for unco-operative neighbors, the emperor's soldiers didn't just kill the enemy fighters. They captured them and marched them back to the capital, where they faced a one-way trip to the top of the Templo Mayor.

The Templo Mayor was located in the center of the city, within a large plaza. In its final form it consisted of a pair of step pyramids side by side. At the top were side-by-side temples, one to the god of rain, the other to Huitzilopochtli. In front of Huitzilopochtli's temple was the sacrificial stone, where priests killed victims with a stone knife. Their bodies were then thrown down 114 steps to the base of the temple.

Moctezuma the First died in 1486. He was succeeded by an emperor named Ahuítzotl (1486–1502). For Ahuítzotl's dedication ceremony of the Templo Mayor, as many as twenty thousand victims were said to have been sacrificed over the course of four days.

In 1502 Ahuítzotl slipped on a stone and hit his head and died. The thirty-four-year-old Moctezuma the Second (grandnephew of Moctezuma the First) became the ninth, and last, Aztec emperor.

MOCTEZUMA II

In his early days Moctezuma had been a priest, and later, a courageous warrior. But he wasn't a very good emperor. Deeply superstitious and out of touch with the real world, he was also indecisive and insecure. When he became emperor, he had all the long-standing servants and advisors of his predecessor put to death to make room for new appointments, who were mostly his relatives. The new advisors in this welcoming workplace environment were too frightened to give him advice or to tell him bad news, because anyone who did so he ordered killed.

Moctezuma II

No one was allowed to look the emperor in the eye, or watch him eat, under penalty of death. Wherever he walked, underlings swept the ground clean in front of him.

To make glum matters gloomier, a series of ominous events increased Moctezuma's fears that the end of the world might be coming. First, the Aztec calendar predicted that this was the year the God of Air planned to return and take back his kingdom. Then a temple was struck by a bolt of lightning. Next came an eclipse. Finally, a comet appeared in the night sky. The emperor, furious that his astrologers and wise men had not predicted these omens ahead of time, had them all killed.

As if Moctezuma didn't have enough to worry about, in 1519 a group of strangely dressed, pale-faced strangers appeared from across the sea.

THE SPANIARDS ARRIVE

Hernán Cortés was a minor nobleman from Spain who sailed to the New World in 1504 in search of fame and fortune, with an emphasis on the fortune part. He set his sights on conquering the interior of the Mexican peninsula.

Cortés arrived on the mainland of Mexico with 508 soldiers, 100 sailors, several hundred Cuban natives, and some African slaves. He also had with him sixteen horses, a

Cortés, impractically dressed for the Mexican climate.

number of ferocious war dogs, some cannons, and some early fire-arms known as arquebuses.

To be sure none of his men would chicken out during this daring mission, Cortés burned most of his ships as soon as they landed. Now there was no turning back.

They began the trek toward the interior of Mexico. Cortés's typical opener, upon encountering any native peoples, was to read a "Requirement" out loud to them. In Spanish. A language they did not speak. Here's a translation of his standard how d'ya do:

> *I implore you to recognize the Church as a lady and in the name of the Pope take the King as lord of this land and obey his mandates. If you do not do it . . . the deaths and injuries that you will receive from here on will be your own fault and not that of his majesty nor of the gentlemen that accompany me.*

As Cortés and his men made their way inland, they read their Requirement, converted some natives, and stole whatever gold they could find from their towns. And then they continued their march toward Tenochtitlán, which is where they believed the *serious* gold was. As they passed a night in the Aztec city of Cholula, Cortés heard a rumor (probably untrue) that someone was plotting to attack the Spaniards. He ordered his soldiers to act first. They slaughtered everyone in the city and burned it to the ground. Then they kept going.

Cortés formed some shrewd alliances with enemies of the

Aztec who were tired of paying tribute to Tenochtitlán, notably the Tlaxcala (tlash-KAH-lah). A group of Tlaxcala warriors joined his army as it marched toward the capital.

MOCTEZUMA'S MISSTEPS

Meanwhile, Moctezuma's spies had delivered the news to the emperor about the appearance of these pale, smelly men wearing funny metal hats and riding enormous deer. (No one had ever seen a horse before.) And worse, these strangers were marching toward the city.

Moctezuma retired to his inner sanctum to think over what he should do. His advisors recommended that he have these foreigners killed. But Moctezuma hesitated. What if Cortés was the God of Air? The god's arrival had been foretold!

Moctezuma sent messengers to the Spaniards. The messengers presented the strangers with luxurious gifts, and then told them to please go away. Unfortunately, some of the gifts were made of gold, which only made the Spaniards more eager to enter the city. They stayed put. At long last, the emperor invited the strangers into the city as his guests. Big mistake.

The Spaniards, who hadn't bathed or had a decent meal in months, were astonished as they entered the magnificent city. And then Moctezuma himself appeared, wearing brilliant-colored robes and festooned with feathers and lots of Aztec bling. His jaguar-skin sandals, encrusted with gemstones, had undersides of gold. (The Spaniards noted the gold part.) Minions swept

Cortés and Moctezuma meet. This will not end well.

the stone pavement in front of the emperor as he approached the visitors.

The Spaniards got a tour of Moctezuma's palace, with its bird sanctuary and its zoo full of wild beasts and venomous creatures, including a snake "with the castanets in its tail."[1]

Then Moctezuma gave them a tour of the Templo Mayor. The strangers were horrified to see the stacks of human skulls, to smell the stench of burnt human hearts, and to meet the blood-covered priests.

They stayed as Moctezuma's guests for several weeks. The Aztec were baffled by the foreigners' nattering on about gold, which the

....
1   Castanets are handheld thingummies that go clackety-clack in rhythm to Spanish dancing.

Aztec thought not nearly as impressive as, say, jade, or exotic bird feathers. (The Aztec word for gold is *teocuitlatl*, pronounced tay-o-quit-LAH-tel. It translates to "excrement of the gods.")

The imperious Cortés demanded that human sacrifices cease and that the Aztec start worshipping the Christian god. Moctezuma was not used to taking orders, and ignored him. Relations between the conquistadors and their host went downhill fast. Before long, Cortés did the unthinkable: He had his men take Moctezuma as a hostage. The news quickly spread throughout Tenochtitlán.

The temple drums began to beat. Several thousand angry Aztec warriors in full battle array answered the call to arms.

A ferocious battle ensued. The far-outnumbered Spaniards hoped to scare the Aztec warriors with their horses and cannons and arquebuses. But it took a lot to scare an Aztec warrior. Cortés's men and their allies retreated behind the walls of the palace. Cortés urged Moctezuma to address the crowd to tell them to back off. Moctezuma came to the balcony and gave a speech. According to Spanish accounts, someone in the crowd threw a stone, which struck the emperor. Then someone threw another. (In the Mexica version of the story, Moctezuma was killed by the Spanish.) He died (or was killed) three days later.

After more fierce fighting, Cortés and his soldiers were forced to flee for their lives. On their way out, some of the Spaniards ransacked the emperor's treasure room and filled their pockets with gold and jewels. Many of them fell into the canals while fleeing, and sank like stones.

A few months later the Spaniards and their allies returned with more soldiers and surrounded the city. They staged a siege, during which an epidemic of smallpox killed untold numbers of Aztec. Perhaps believing their gods had abandoned them, the sick and demoralized people of Tenochtitlán finally surrendered.

Cortés and other Spaniards set up shop in the smoldering remains of the city and began to rebuild it. The conquerors dismantled many buildings that hadn't been destroyed and used the stones to build new buildings. Temples became churches. The rebuilt city became part of New Spain. The Aztec survivors adopted some Spanish customs and beliefs, but kept many old traditions.

The once glorious Aztec civilization had lasted for less than two hundred years.

BACK TO THE PRESENT

Since the unearthing of that huge round stone in 1978, more Aztec discoveries have been made. In 2006 workers digging the foundation of a new building uncovered a twelve-ton rectangular image of the Aztec earth goddess. In 2017 another giant temple and part of a ball court were discovered underneath a hotel.

Since the chance discovery of the Templo Mayor, archaeologists have excavated large areas of its ruins. More still lie twenty-five feet below the ground. Today archaeologists work in areas all over Mexico City. So much more of this city's remarkable history remains to be discovered.

Chapter Fourteen

GRAVE CONSIDERATIONS

🔲 THE DISCOVERY

The year is 1989. The place, downtown New York City. Construction is due to start on a new, thirty-four-story federal office building. As always happens before anyone digs a big hole in the ground in the middle of the city, contractors are called in to do what's called an environmental impact study. They check out old city records to be sure there's nothing of historical interest in the ground.

It's just a formality. No one expects them to find anything. They uncover an old map from the eighteenth century that indicates that part of the site of the new building overlaps the site of what used to be known as the city's "Commons," which was what they called an open, public space. And some old documents say that in the 1600s, when the city was first settled, the Commons had been a place for grazing cows. By the 1700s some public buildings had been constructed in the area of the Commons, including a poorhouse. The map suggests that there may have been a burial ground here, too, for people of African descent.

But that's all in the distant past. In the nineteenth and twentieth centuries, Manhattan rapidly expanded. New buildings went up where the Commons used to be. Water and electric pipes were laid deep below the streets.

And it's common knowledge that in most cemeteries, bodies are buried six feet beneath the ground. In New York City, the "subbasements" of most buildings are dug twenty feet down. Even if any human remains *had* once been buried here, there's no way they can have survived after all these centuries of building and hole digging and pipe laying.

Still, by law the building owner—in this case the federal government—needs to make sure. The contractors call in archaeologists and ask them to dig around a bit.

Almost immediately, they unearth an eighteenth-century coffin.

PiLED UP AND PROTECTED

The construction project was put on hold. To everyone's surprise, more and more coffins were uncovered. The old map turned out to be accurate. It indicated that this area had been the site of what was called the "Negros Burial Ground." But how had the bones survived all those centuries of buildings?

After more probing, researchers learned that back in the eighteenth century, the Commons had been in a low-lying area. As new building foundations were dug nearby, the soil that had been removed was dumped onto the Commons, burying the grave site beneath about twenty feet of earth. Because it was a burial ground for Black people, most of them enslaved, white mapmakers never bothered to mark the location. But all that piled-up soil protected the remains of the people buried there.

Can you find the area marked COMMON? That's where the burial ground is located.

The discovery of the burial ground was made public. Archaeologists specializing in human remains carefully removed the remains of dozens of people. A year into the project, the remains of nearly four hundred people were recovered. But despite working long hours day after day, the excavators faced mounting pressure to finish the job quickly so that the construction could resume.

When news about the government wanting to resume construction went public, there was a storm of public protest. After multiple meetings with members of the Black community, the federal government property owners announced that they would cancel plans to build on that section of the site. A modified version of the building would be completed in 1994, leaving the area of the burial ground untouched.

Excavations continued. African descendant community leaders and scholars were (eventually) put in charge of the project. For years afterward, historians, archaeologists, and anthropologists at Howard University and other universities would examine every bone fragment and artifact found at the site, under the direction of anthropologist Michael L. Blakey. After being examined, the bones would later be reburied at the site, and a memorial and museum built.

MANHATTAN'S DUTCH BEGINNINGS

In the 1620s Dutch fur traders established a colony on the southern tip of Manhattan and called it New Amsterdam. The area had forests and meadows and ponds, and had been inhabited for centuries by the Lenape people. The first Dutch governor, Peter Minuit, made a deal with the Lenape. In exchange for some Dutch coins and trinkets, he believed he had bought Manhattan. The Lenape believed they were agreeing to share the land. That "misunderstanding" would lead to decades of violent clashes between the native people and the white settlers.

By 1626 New Amsterdam had grown to a small village of about three hundred people, mostly of European descent. That same year, eleven enslaved African men were brought to the colony. Labor remained in short supply, and the number of workers in bondage gradually increased. Between 1644 and 1664 the number of enslaved people in New Amsterdam tripled.

BUILDING A BARRICADE

In 1653 the British and Dutch were at war with each other. Enslaved Black laborers built a high wall along New Amsterdam's northern border to protect the settlement. Today the wall is gone, but the area is called Wall Street.

NEW AMSTERDAM BECOMES NEW YORK

In 1664 the Dutch governor was forced to hand over the colony of New Amsterdam to the British.[1] Its name was changed to New York. The British, in need of ever more labor in the fast-growing settlement, brought more—and more—slaves from Africa and the Caribbean to New York. By 1700 New York had become a bustling port town with about five thousand people. At least seven hundred of them were free or enslaved Black people.

THE BURIAL GROUND: BEGINNINGS

As in many other colonial cities, British officials banned Black New Yorkers from being buried in the same grounds as

....
1   Long story, but the deal between the British and the Dutch was basically a swap. On the other side of the world in a place called the Banda Islands, the two nations were fighting over control of nutmeg—yes, nutmeg. The trading of that spice was quite lucrative. After brutal fighting there, the two powers signed a treaty. The Dutch got all the nutmeg plantations. The British got Manhattan, and they weren't all that excited about the trade.

white New Yorkers. So Black people created their own burial ground about a mile north of the southern end of Manhattan. The site was beyond the city's wall, and though they didn't receive official permission for it, no one much cared, because it was on land no one wanted. Some of the dead that were buried there were free Blacks, but most were enslaved. Later, during the American Revolution, the burial ground would also be used to bury prisoners of war, both British and American, black and white.

BLACK PEOPLE BUILD THE CITY

In the first half of the 1700s, enslaved New Yorkers performed a variety of jobs. Enslaved women cleaned, cooked, shopped, washed, sewed, and carried water. They also looked after white children. Most men performed manual labor, although in wealthy homes some were house servants. Some enslaved men became highly skilled at trades. They worked alongside their enslavers as potters, carpenters, blacksmiths, and coopers (people who make and fix wooden barrels). Many who could read and write worked for merchants, attorneys, and physicians. Sometimes slaveowners hired out their slaves to the city to work on public projects such as building dams, roads, and canals. Unlike in the southern colonies, where slave quarters were often separate from the main house, most enslaved people in New York lived under the same roof as their enslavers. They often slept in cellars, attics, or kitchens, where it could be infernally hot in summer and unbearably cold in winter.

With the growing population of white people in the city, life for Black New Yorkers under British rule became increasingly strict.

Enslaved people had fewer rights than they'd had under Dutch rule. They were not allowed to leave their owner's residence without permission. It was illegal for them to gather in groups of four or more (because white New Yorkers were afraid they might be planning to revolt). And of course, every enslaved person faced the constant fear of being sold again and parted from their loved ones.

Still, enslaved people managed to defy the laws that restricted their movements. Because skilled labor was in such high demand, and because many white enslavers were away a lot, Black people were able to meet at the water pumps and in taverns. They gathered together to bury their dead, usually at night. They also found

A rare view of a house servant (left) and dockside laborers. Enslaved Africans toiled in New Amsterdam from its earliest beginnings.

ways to celebrate their cultural identity through music, songs, and religious gatherings (including funerals).

THE LiVES THEY LED

In some graves, infants were found cradled in their mothers' arms. There were graves that contained objects people had been buried with, such as beads, buttons, coins, rings, and tobacco pipes. Some skeletons showed front teeth that had been filed into distinctive shapes—pointed or hourglass shaped. The shaping of teeth had been a custom in many West African cultures, and helped archaeologists determine where in Africa the person may have come from.

Diseases and hard work left marks on people's bones. Skeletal remains showed signs of rickets, fractures, and malnutrition. Thickened ridges on some bones attested to a lifetime of lifting heavy loads. A damaged spine indicated that the person had— quite literally—done backbreaking work. The remains of one young woman were found to contain a musket ball in the rib cage, which likely was what had killed her. Perhaps she had tried to escape slavery, or join a rebellion.

NEW YORK CiTY AND THE AMERICAN REVOLUTiON

The American Revolution began in 1775. Both sides—the British and the American colonists—faced a serious shortage of soldiers. In the early years of the war, slaves were not permitted to enlist on the side of the American colonial army. But then the British governor of Virginia, Lord Dunmore, declared that all slaves willing

The proclamation by John Murray, fourth Earl of Dunmore.

to fight on the side of England would be freed after the war. Enslaved people fled from their enslavers in southern territories and streamed into Virginia to fight on the side of the British.

That made the American colonists rethink their policy. State by state, some began enlisting black soldiers, who joined up with the promise that they would be freed after the war ended.

British troops captured New York City in 1776. The British would occupy the city for the next seven years. In 1779 the British general Henry Clinton issued a proclamation. It offered freedom to all slaves willing to flee their masters and join up with the British in the north.

Hoping for liberation after the war, thousands of runaways from the south streamed into New York during the British occupation. Both men and women worked as porters, sailors, cooks, and seamstresses.

The very first skeleton unearthed in 1989 turned out to be the remains of a male soldier. Although any fabric the grave had once contained had long since decomposed, excavators found buttons that showed he'd been buried in a British naval uniform at the time of the American Revolution.

BOARDING BRITISH BOATS

The Americans won the war. A treaty was signed in 1783. In accordance with the terms of the treaty, the British were allowed to evacuate the American territories peacefully, so long as they promised not to carry away any American property. In George Washington's eyes, this "property" included slaves.[2]

But General Clinton honored his promise to free Black people who had served on the British side. As he explained to Washington, he could not in good conscience return former slaves to the Americans, as many of the former slaves would be seriously punished or even executed for fleeing from their enslavers. That, he said, would be a "dishonorable Violation of the public Faith."

Black people flocked to the port to board British ships bound for somewhere—anywhere—in the British Empire. General Clinton ordered that careful records be kept of the Black people they

....
2   Yes, George Washington was a slaveowner. He owned 316 people at the time of his death.

transported, in case the British might be asked to pay compensation to American enslavers for "lost property" at a later date. The British created a detailed registry of over four thousand men, women, and children. In the register, columns listed the person's name, former master, the ship they were on, and a brief physical description. Some of these descriptions shed light on both the passenger and the record-keeper: "fine boy," "likely rascal," and "nearly worn out."

In a letter to a friend, an annoyed Washington wrote, "I have discovered enough to convince me that the slaves which have absconded from their masters will never be restored."

SLAVERY IN THE NORTH

Are you surprised to hear that there were so many enslaved people living in New York City? Most history books tend to focus on slavery in the southern colonies, but, in fact, by 1703 *40 percent* of white homes in Manhattan included enslaved Black people.

After the American Revolution, because northern states did not depend as much on slavery for their economy as the cotton-producing southern states, it was easier for white people in the North to follow their consciences and join the fight against slavery. Slavery was abolished in New York in 1827. (In the South, and throughout the United States, slavery would not be abolished until after the Civil War ended, in 1865.)

BACK TO THE PRESENT

The burial ground closed in 1795. By then the city had expanded northward and that land had become valuable. As white developers built on the land that had once been the Commons, a new Black burial ground was established near what today is Manhattan's Lower East Side.

No one is sure how many more remains are still buried at the site, but estimates have ranged from 10,000 to 20,000 people. The original burial ground area may have covered more than six acres. In 2003 the bones that had been excavated were reburied. The remaining graves may remain undisturbed. The federal office building was erected on part of the original site, and a visiting center was created for the ground floor. Another part of the site has been left as open space, with a pavilion and a Wall of Remembrance. Today special permission must be granted for any new construction above the entire site of the original burial ground. The African Burial Ground was named a US National Monument in 2006.

Chapter Fifteen

DEAD IN A DITCH

THE DISCOVERY

The year is 1991. The place, a high mountain pass in the Alps near the border between Italy and Austria. A German couple named Helmut and Erika Simon is out hiking. It has been a warm summer and some of the ice and snow has melted. They approach a gully. It's about 131 feet long and about 10 feet deep. In the gully, they spot what appears to be a dead body. They move closer to investigate. It is indeed the remains of a man. He lies face-down, stuck fast in the ice below his waist.

The hikers notify the mountain rescue team. Because the body has been found very close to the border, both Austrian and Italian police arrive on the scene. A team with pickaxes and drills finally manages to extract the body from the ice. At first, everyone assumes he is a mountaineer who died in an accident. They

The Iceman as he was first discovered.

transport the body to the medical examiner's office, along with the other items that had been found near it. Rather quickly the medical technicians realize the situation before them is unusual. One hint—the tools and other objects found near the body are not . . . modern. Archaeologists are called in.

As it turns out, the well-preserved body has been lying there quite a bit longer than anyone could have imagined.

Over five thousand years, to be exact.

NOT JUST ANY BODY

With growing excitement, archaeologists realized they were staring at the oldest naturally preserved mummy ever found. They named the man Ötzi (which rhymes with "Tootsie"). An examination of

Ötzi commenced, along with a study of his possessions, which included his ax, a bow, a dagger, his clothes, and other curious items. For the next twenty-five-plus years, teams of international researchers would examine every part of Ötzi, all the way down to his cellular DNA. He would become the most-studied human being . . . ever.

What's remarkable and exciting about Ötzi is that though he's a mummy, he's not like the mummies of ancient Egypt. Those had been gutted and dried out and embalmed and wrapped up to preserve them for the afterlife. Ötzi is what is known disturbingly as a "wet mummy," which means he was preserved naturally and quickly; in his case, by dying and quickly freezing before too much decomposition set in. And because he'd ended up in the trench, his body had been relatively protected from damage by the huge moving glaciers that scraped the mountainside above him.

Even after he'd lain there for 5,300 years, scientists found that most of Ötzi's insides were well preserved. Which means they could analyze the contents of his stomach and identify what he'd eaten for his last meal. They could map his genes and determine the color of his eyes (brown), the color of his hair (also brown), his blood type, and even some diseases that had ailed him.

SOME SECRETS REVEALED

Ötzi was somewhere in his forties when he died, which would have been a fairly ripe old age for someone from his era. He'd been about five feet, four inches tall. The strong muscles and

An artist's reconstruction of what Otzi may have looked like.

bones of his legs indicated that he walked a lot and carried heavy loads, leading to speculation that he might have been a shepherd. Minerals in his teeth revealed what was in his drinking water, so scientists could figure out where he'd lived as a child.

His body was decorated with over fifty tattoos. They weren't the kind you make with a needle; they were a series of cuts into which someone had rubbed charcoal. The tattoos don't seem to have been decorative, because most of them were on his lower body and would have been covered by his clothing. They were probably there as a guide for acupuncture, a procedure for soothing pain. Before Ötzi's discovery, scientists hadn't known that acupuncture had been practiced so long ago, and in Ötzi's part of the world.

ÖTZI'S LAST DAY

Here's how Ötzi began the last day of his life. He woke up and dressed in his cold-weather gear: goatskin leggings, a deerskin tunic, and a heavy grass cape, stitched together with thread made of animal sinews. He stuffed his leather footies with grass to insulate his feet from the cold, and pulled on a bearskin hat.

Then he breakfasted on a hefty meal: greasy, wild-goat steak and some sort of grain-based thing, perhaps bread.[1] Gross, you say? Ötzi knew it was important to eat enough calories to keep from freezing as he trekked into the mountains. And chewing on goat gristle is just the ticket.

Next he slung on his gear: a copper ax with a wooden handle, a bow, a quiver of arrows with flint points, and a flint dagger. Inside a pouch, he carried two kinds of mushroom. One, known as tinder fungus, ignites easily when it's dried and is used to start a fire. The other, known as birch polyspore, has antiseptic power. If you tie it around a wound with a piece of grass, it acts like a Neolithic Band-Aid.

SNEAK ATTACK

Ötzi suffered from some troublesome ailments, including terrible teeth, advanced gum disease, ongoing diarrhea due to parasitic worms in his stomach, and high concentrations of poisonous arsenic in his system. Because arsenic dust is produced when heating and extracting copper from rock, scientists believe he may have been a coppersmith. His DNA showed evidence of a disease-causing bacteria called Borrelia, which would make him the earliest known sufferer of Lyme disease. He also had fleas.

....

1   His stomach also had trace amounts of a poisonous plant called bracken. Scientists think he might have wrapped his lunch in this large fern. Doing so regularly may have caused some chronic stomach problems.

But fleas turned out to have been the least of Ötzi's problems. A few days before he died, he'd been involved in a fight, and it had been a nasty one. He suffered a deep cut on his right hand, as though he'd tried to ward off a knife-wielding attacker. It had begun to heal.

It took a few years of studying Ötzi before an especially observant radiologist noticed Ötzi's most serious health complaint, revealed in an X-ray. Buried in Ötzi's left shoulder was a flint arrowhead.

The shaft of the arrow itself was missing. Someone had pulled it out and left the broken-off arrowhead in Ötzi's shoulder. Could Ötzi himself have tried to pull the arrow out? Or had it been pulled out by his attacker, who wanted his arrow back?

More tests were done, and more details emerged. Ötzi had been shot from behind. The location of the arrow suggests that it would have pierced a major artery. He probably bled to death in minutes.

He had also sustained a severe head injury. Had his attacker knocked him over the head after shooting him with the arrow, to be sure he was dead? Or had he dumped Ötzi off a cliff while Otzi was still sort of alive, so that he banged his head when he landed in the trench?

Whatever happened, and how—Ötzi's cause of death was now clear. He was murdered.

CLUES TO THE COPPER AGE

Ötzi lived during what's known as the Copper Age in Europe. Flint and stone tools and weapons were just starting to be replaced by metal ones. And copper was one of the earliest metals. It's a mineral, and easy to find. It's relatively soft and bendable, and can be beaten into different shapes without having to melt it down (although eventually people did that, too).

Ötzi's discovery is especially exciting because it added to what little is known about everyday life during the Copper Age in Europe. It was a time of transition—the hunter-gatherer lifestyle of the Neolithic era was changing over to widespread adoption of farming. Ötzi helped us learn more about human cultures in this part of the world.

BACK TO THE PRESENT

Today Ötzi's body lies in a carefully climate-controlled room in the South Tyrol Museum of Archaeology, in northern Italy. Before his body was discovered, archaeologists had had very little

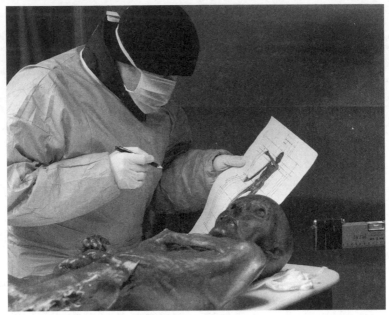

Ötzi under examination.

to study in the way of Copper Age artifacts—a few flint tools, some shards of pottery, parts of skeletons. So imagine how much he has added to our understanding of life during Ötzi's time. And tests on his body continue. He has lots more to teach us.

Chapter Sixteen

SKELETON KEY

THE DiSCOVERY

The year is 2012. The place, a city called Leicester—it rhymes with "pester"—in the middle of England. A filmmaker named Philippa Langley has come here to research a new project. She's working on a screenplay based on the life of a medieval English king named Richard III. He lived during the Middle Ages in England, and was killed in a battle—now called the Battle of Bosworth—in 1485. Also, he's gone down in history as one of England's nastiest rulers. High on the long list of evil deeds he's accused of: He supposedly murdered two children—the rightful heirs to the British throne—and then seized it for himself.

Philippa wants to change the way Richard's story has been told. She's the secretary of the Scottish branch of a group called the Richard III Society. The socicty has chapters all over the world.

Richard III, in what is now considered one of his more accurate-looking portraits.

Members of this group—sometimes referred to as "Ricardians"—believe that Richard III was not a wicked king. They think he has been given an undeservedly bad reputation by history.

Philippa has come to the city of Leicester because she's located a medieval-era document that says that after Richard was killed in the battle, his body was flung over a horse and transported fifteen miles to this city, and that the body was then buried in a church called Greyfriars. But the church was destroyed in the sixteenth century. So there's the small hitch that no one knows exactly where the church's ruins are. Quite a few archaeologists are interested in finding those ruins. Philippa has decided to take it one step further—if they can locate the ruins of the church, somewhere beneath these bustling streets, perhaps they can find the remains of Richard himself.

She has also found a map that was created in 1741, almost three hundred years after Richard died. It shows that a mansion was built on the site of what *might* have once been the old church, and that the mansion had a large formal garden. The mansion and gardens are gone, but there's now a parking lot (which English people call a car park) in the very place that the garden used to be.

Philippa walks into this parking lot. And then something

strange happens. She is suddenly seized with a feeling—a certainty, really—that she's standing on Richard's grave.

Philippa has excellent marketing skills. She puts the word out to her Ricardian group that she believes—no, is certain—that Richard is buried here. She calls the project "Looking for Richard." Money pours in. In a remarkably short time, she raises the funds to start an excavation in that parking lot. (In case you're wondering—this is not the way archaeological excavations are typically funded.)

The excavation is headed up by an unconvinced archaeologist from nearby Leicester University named Richard Buckley. He does not think Philippa's strategy for deciding where to dig for Richard is very . . . scientific. He does not think they're going to find Richard's grave. In fact, he rates the odds as "not seriously considered possible." Still, he *would* like to locate the ruins of the long-lost Greyfriars church, and he has some independent evidence that the ruins *could* be in the vicinity of Philippa's parking lot. Thanks to the funds Philippa has raised, there's money enough to assemble a team, and in August of 2012, the "Looking for Richard" team begins its excavation.

On the first day, a construction worker operating a small backhoe carefully removes the top layer of pavement to create two long, shallow trenches. Now the archaeologists can begin their dig.

On the second day, at eight o'clock in the morning, the archaeologists find some human bones in one of the trenches.

Digging in that trench stops. Paleoanthropologists—archaeologists who specialize in excavating human remains—take over. They don long-sleeved white onesies and gloves, so as not to contaminate the bones, and begin the painstaking task of uncovering the skeleton. Meanwhile, digging commences in the other trench.

Almost immediately they uncover the ruins of an old building. Could it be the church?

In case you're wondering—the odds of making two such discoveries this quickly are, well, extremely unusual in the field of archaeology.

TREACHEROUS TiMES

Why even *is* there a group called the Richard III Society? Who actually cares whether this minor medieval ruler, who reigned for just over two years, was given an undeservedly bad reputation?

This is where William Shakespeare enters the story.[1]

One hundred or so years after the real Richard was killed at the Battle of Bosworth, Shakespeare wrote a fictional play about him. To some extent Shakespeare's play *Richard III* is based on facts: Richard was the last monarch in a royal line known as the Plantagenets. His successor, Henry VII, was the *first* of the royal line known as the Tudors. And Shakespeare worked for the Tudors. So Ricardians believe that Shakespeare was under certain pressure to paint King Richard as a Plantagenet villain to please his Tudor employers. In Shakespeare's play, after King Edward, Richard's older brother, dies, Richard orders the murder of Edward's two young sons, who are the rightful heirs to his throne. His own nephews.

....
1   Yes, *that* William Shakespeare.

Did this actually happen? In real life, Edward IV, Richard's brother, did die suddenly. And Richard was appointed the "Lord Protector" of the two young princes, meaning he was the grown-up in charge until his nephews Edward V, aged twelve, or his younger brother Richard, aged nine, became old enough to rule. And it's true that the young princes disappeared.

In Shakespeare's play, King Richard III is portrayed as a scheming tyrant who murders his way to the throne.

What gets murky is that Shakespeare and others from Team Tudor assumed that Richard ordered the deaths of the two young princes. Ricardians think Richard had nothing to do with their disappearance. Hmmm.

THE MAKING OF THIS MONARCH

In real life, Richard Plantagenet was born at Fotheringhay Castle in 1452, the twelfth of thirteen children in a family line called the House of York. He was the fourth-oldest son to survive to adulthood and so was considered an extreme long shot to be crowned king. His was not what anyone would describe as a happy childhood. His grandfather had been beheaded. His father and one brother were killed in a battle when he was eight. Later, his brother, the king, had another of their brothers executed for treason.

Physically, Richard had some issues. Just how severe they were depends on whether you believe the Ricardians or the pro-Tudor people. Shakespeare painted him as a "lump of foul deformity," or, in kinder terms, a person with a crooked back. He added a withered arm for good measure. Was this Tudor propaganda? In Shakespeare's day, physical deformity was often believed—wrongly—to be a sign of a deformed mind. The Ricardians don't believe Richard had a humped back at all.

DASTARDLY DEEDS

Richard did do some shocking things. He married the widow of a man he'd had a hand in killing. He greenlighted the execution

One artist's rendition of the princes in the tower—the ones that disappeared while under their uncle's protection.

of his brother George when George was accused of treason. And then when his brother King Edward unexpectedly died, Richard had King Edward's marriage declared invalid, which meant that Edward's sons/Richard's nephews had no legal right to become kings. And then the nephews disappeared.

Monstrous? Or simply . . . run-of-the-mill ruthless?

Where historians disagree is how much of all this was ordinary medieval royal shenanigans, and how much was especially wicked behavior.

Members of Team Richard point to the good stuff he did, like cutting taxes and supporting churches and promising better times to come. He was an okay husband, and also quite loyal to his brother-king (while his brother lived), and he was rewarded with land up north to preside over. As for all the throne-grabbing and disappearing of relatives, one could argue that he was just trying to survive in a competitive world.

Wherever one stands on that debate today, there were a lot of people in Richard's day who disagreed with the way he seized the throne. Some of those people fled to France, and there they recognized Henry Tudor as the rightful king.

Richard had been king for just a little over two years when Henry Tudor and his army invaded England in 1485. The two forces met about fifteen miles southeast of Leicester and fought the Battle of Bosworth. It was the medieval kind of battle, with mounted knights swinging swords, flinging spears, and thrusting with daggers and halberds. Richard was killed in that battle. Henry Tudor became Henry VII, the new king.

A halberd is a nasty medieval-era weapon. It's a six-foot-long spear that also has an ax-like blade at the end.

King Henry ordered Richard's bloodied corpse put on display for two days, "laide openly that every man might se and luke upon him," so that everyone would be sure he was actually dead.

In this nineteenth-century depiction of the 1485 Battle of Bosworth, the Earl of Richmond, soon-to-be King Henry VII, is about to dispatch King Richard. Very unlikely that it happened this way.

But then what? Some accounts claim that the body was thrown into the nearby river by an angry mob, and was gone forever.

THE COMEBACK KING

Soon after Philippa's team uncovered the skeleton—which they called "Skeleton 1"—archaeologists could clearly see that the bones belonged to a male adult. And that he'd had a curved spine. And that there was evidence that Skeleton 1 had sustained severe battle wounds. Could this really be Richard?

A study published in December 2014, headed up by scientists at the University of Leicester, confirmed that on the basis of radiocarbon dating, DNA tests, and bone analysis, the skeleton was almost certainly that of Richard III. The scientists also

A POSITIVE ID

Dr. Turi King, a scientist in the University of Leicester's Department of Genetics, and Dr. Jo Appleby, from the University's School of Archaeology and Ancient History, led the excavation and analysis of Skeleton 1's bones. They compared ancient DNA extracted from the bones and teeth of Skeleton 1 to those of two of Richard's living descendants—two fourteenth cousins twice removed—who agreed to be tested. Dr. King found that the DNA precisely matched their samples. The bones were Richard's.

concluded that although the skeleton had a curved spine, Richard hadn't been a hunchback, the way Shakespeare portrayed him. But Richard's skeleton did show clear signs of scoliosis, which is a condition that causes the spine to curve to one side, and which makes one shoulder higher than the other.

After analyzing chemicals found in the teeth, bones, and ribs, scientists determined that Richard III ate well, which in medieval times meant a lot of meat and fish. His diet was filled with fancy delicacies like swan, crane, and heron. He had a slender frame, and would have stood about five feet, nine inches if not for his curved spine. He probably had blond hair and blue eyes.

In the battle, he sustained at least eleven wounds, including two nasty cuts on his head, either of which might have killed him.

Digging up a king.

One was a huge gash at the base of his skull. It might have been made with a halberd. The other wound was at the top of his head, which may have been made with a dagger or a sword. Because none of the wounds showed signs of healing, they had to have been inflicted at the time of death, or possibly right after.

News outlets around the world breathlessly reported about the discovery of "the king in the car park."

BACK TO THE PRESENT

Once it was clear that the bones belonged to Richard, a battle over where—and whether—to rebury Richard's remains was fought on a Battle-of-Bosworth scale. One group called the Plantagenet Alliance collected thirty thousand signatures protesting the reburial of this "evil" monarch. Another group, descendants of the House of York, wanted him buried at—no shocker here—York. But finally the High Court weighed in, and in March of 2015, Richard's bones were buried in Leicester Cathedral in a grand ceremony fit for a king. The debate continues to rage about Richard III's true character.

Chapter Seventeen

THE CHAMBER OF SECRETS

THE DISCOVERY

It's September 13, 2013. The place, just outside the city of Johannesburg, in South Africa. Two friends named Rick Hunter and Steven Tucker explore a cave. This area is known as the "Cradle of Humankind," because back in the first half of the twentieth century, many important fossils of ancient humans were found in the many cave systems here. Ever since, paleoanthropologists have explored the area thoroughly. Most of them think all the fossils that can be found *have* been found around here, and have moved on to other parts of Africa. But Rick and Steve have a geologist friend named Pedro Boshoff. Pedro works for a paleoanthropologist named Lee Berger. Lee has asked Pedro to tell his caver friends to be on the lookout for fossils of early humans whenever they go caving. Because you never know, right?

Rick and Steve explore caves for fun. They both have day jobs. Rick is a construction worker. Steve is an accountant. Both are slim and wiry.

The two enter a well-known cave system called the Rising Star. Steve wants to show Rick a great climb called Dragon's Back. It takes about fifteen minutes to get to the climb, and the going is difficult. First, they make their way through what cavers call a "squeeze," two walls of rock so narrow that even skinny guys like Rick and Steve can get through it only by inching sideways. Then they have to drop down and shinny along on their bellies through a low passage. It's so narrow, they have to squinch along with one arm tight against their side, the other outstretched, like Superman flying through the air. Not everyone would consider this fun, but Steve and Rick are cavers, so they do.

They arrive at Dragon's Back. It's a jagged, rocky ridge about as high as a three-story building. Because they're experienced cavers and in great physical condition, they both climb nimbly up the pointed, slippery rocks.

At the top there's a gap. They leap across it onto a narrow ledge.

Rick wants to take a video of the gorgeous rock formations. Steve spies a small opening near their feet. To get out of Rick's shot, he lowers himself into it.

And then he realizes his feet haven't touched anything. Beneath him is empty space—it's a long, vertical shaft.

This is why cavers are unusual sorts of people. A sensible person would haul himself right back out of a narrow shaft that extends downward who knows how far into pitch-blackness. But Steve is a caver, so instead, he decides to investigate. And Rick follows. They inch their way down, down, down the shaft. At one point the shaft becomes very tight—not much wider than the length of your pencil. It's so tight that even skinny people like Steve and Rick can barely squeeze through. This narrow passage extends down forty feet—that's about the length of a telephone pole. At the bottom, there's a short drop to the floor of a chamber.

It's pitch-black in the chamber. But the lights on their helmets reveal flecks of white scattered around the floor. The white things are bones, and there are a lot of them. Steve and Rick aren't trained archaeologists, but they wonder if these bones could be human. They don't touch anything, but they take lots of video footage.

Some of the bones found in the chamber, after they'd been sorted and reassembled.

Later that same evening, Lee Berger hears a knock on his front door. It's nine thirty on a Friday night, an unusual hour for paleoanthropologists to receive visitors. When Lee opens the door, he sees Rick, Steve, and their friend Pedro on his doorstep. They look excited.

"Lee, you're really going to want to see this," says Pedro.

RELATIVE TERMS

A *hominid* is a term that describes all members of the primate family, including apes and humans. A *hominin* is a term for humans and humanlike relatives that have more in common with modern humans than with modern apes and other primates.

A BIG JOB FOR SMALL SCIENTISTS

Lee looked at the pictures Steve and Rick had taken in the cave chamber. He believed that the bones were almost certainly those of hominins. In this line of work, a paleoanthropologist can spend decades searching and in his or her entire career can feel lucky to find a single fragment of a bone. Fossils of some early human species can be so rare, much of what has been found for them could fit comfortably in your lunch bag, with room for your sandwich. That's why Lee's eyes were bulging. These pictures showed *hundreds* of bones.

Lee realized they had to act quickly. An incredible find like this wouldn't remain secret for long, and the cave needed to be protected from curiosity seekers. It would take trained archaeologists to carefully map, excavate, and then bring the bones out of the cave for study. But Lee was a large man. There was no way he could shinny through the squeeze and squinch along Superman's Crawl and clamber up Dragon's Back, let alone wriggle his way down the long chute into that chamber. He'd get stuck like a cork. And that was true of most of his senior scientist colleagues. None were slim and athletic enough to make that difficult, thirty-minute journey into the secret chamber.

He needed some small, athletic scientists, and he needed them fast. So he turned to social media.

An unusual *Help Wanted* ad appeared on Lee's Facebook page. He was looking for experienced archaeologists and paleontologists—"Ph.D.'s and senior scientists most welcome"—for a secret project that was to happen right away. Candidates, the ad said, "must be skinny and preferably small. They must not be claustrophobic [afraid of small spaces], they must be fit [athletic], they should have some caving experience; climbing experience would be a bonus." Also, the ad said, "I do not think we will have much money available for pay." All of which translated to: We need scientists with advanced degrees who can fit through a seven-inch space. Also they need to drop everything they're doing to travel to an undisclosed location for at least a month, to do something dangerous and secret. For which they won't be paid.

The post was shared many times. Applications rolled in.

MEASURING UP

Five weeks later Lee had put together a team of six scientists. He'd conducted dozens of interviews with qualified applicants. All six

Becca Peixotto and Marina Elliott, two of the first scientists to enter the chamber.

scientists happened to be young and female. Some were experienced cavers. Some were still in graduate school. All had a slightly different area of expertise. And all of them were thrilled to have landed the job. Lee dubbed them the "Underground Astronauts." To prepare for her interview, one of the scientists, the five-foot, two-inch Alia Gurtov, set two chairs back-to-back, seven inches apart, "to see if I could make it through." She could.

About three weeks later, a group of paleoanthropologists, geologists, and other scientists, including the six Underground Astronauts, arrived in South Africa and set up camp outside the entrance to the cave. They established an aboveground command center, where Lee and his colleagues would stand by to receive the specimens. They readied the cave for the excavation. Steve and Rick and other amateur cavers helped set up miles of wires, cameras, lights, pulleys, and air-quality meters inside the cave, all along the route and down into the chamber. Lee established strict safety procedures. The command center would be able to monitor every part of the route on closed-circuit TVs. The Underground Astronauts went through rigorous safety training.

Finally it was time. The excavators formed teams of three,

Lee Berger (sitting at the computer) with colleagues at the aboveground command center.

working two-hour shifts.[1] Marina Elliott, Becca Peixotto, and Hannah Morris were the first team to enter the cave.

Down in the chamber it was quiet and beautiful. "Once you were in there you didn't want to leave," said Alia. It was also teeming with bones. Over the next three weeks, the scientists marked the locations of fossils, then carefully removed and bagged the bones and brought them up and out of the caves. Lee and the other experts stood by, ready to receive every specimen as it came out. The most exciting excavation was a skull.

Everyone had questions. Did the fossils belong to hominins?

....

1   Wondering what happened if someone had to go to the bathroom while down in
     the chamber? Of course you are. They had a plastic container down there, in a
     place that was out of view of the closed-circuit cameras.

Two excavators squeezing their way toward the chamber.

Was it a new species of early human? How old were the bones? And how did they get into that cave? Answering those questions would take some time.

PUTTING A PUZZLE TOGETHER

The bones were transported to a university in Johannesburg, where Lee had assembled another group of specialists to study and evaluate them. The scientists divided into groups according to whatever body part was their specialty: One group's was skulls. Another's was hands. Others' were teeth, spines, hips, or feet.

After painstaking evaluations and a big group effort, they made the results public. The bones turned out to belong to a previously unknown species of early human. Lee Berger named it *Homo naledi* (naledi means "star" in the Sotho language). Over

1,550 specimens from at least fifteen different individuals had been recovered from the cave chamber (now known as Dinaledi). It's the largest collection of a single early human species ever found in Africa.

After the specialists pieced together their findings, a physical description of *H. naledi* emerged. Turns out, it was an odd-looking, puzzling combination of human and not-quite-human characteristics. Males were about five feet tall, and weighed about a hundred pounds. Females were a bit shorter and lighter.

H. naledi had a monkey-like face with a small head and a jutting-out jaw. Its upper body was also pretty monkey-like, built to climb and swing from trees. But its lower body was more humanlike. Its hips and legs were built for walking, on feet that look a lot like ours. It probably walked and ran much the way you do.

An artist's reconstruction of *H. naledi*'s head.

The next bombshell occurred when scientists managed to figure out the age of the bones. That happened in 2017. The bones turned out to be much more recent than many people predicted: between 236,000 and 335,000 years old. Which means that *Homo naledi* shared the earth with other species of humans, including *our* species, *Homo sapiens*, the only one to survive to today.

THE ROUTE TO THE CHUTE

Another big question: How did the bones get into the chamber? Could the dead bodies have been dragged there by predators? Or could there have been a flood that washed the bodies into the cave? Based on soil samples and other scientific tests from the area where the bones were found, researchers ruled out both possibilities. Could there have been another way into the cave? None has been found.

Which led to a crazy theory: Perhaps *H. naledi* deliberately disposed of dead bodies by dumping them down the chute. The ritual of burying one's dead is an advanced kind of behavior, usually associated with modern, bigger-brained hominins. The route to the chamber is a long way to lug a dead body, and not an easy one. Can you imagine dragging a deceased relative through Superman's Crawl and up Dragon's Back?[2] That would have required advance planning and group cooperation.

Which raises yet another point. Deep inside the cave, it would have been pitch-black. If the bodies were brought in there intentionally, does that mean *H. naledi*, with its small brain, knew how to make fire? So many questions remain to be answered.

....

2   More than once, some of the cavers laying safety equipment got pantsed while squinching through Superman's Crawl, to the merriment of those monitoring things in the command center.

BACK TO THE PRESENT

In 2017 Rick and Steve discovered another chamber in the same cave system. It's now called the Lesedi Chamber, and it contains another sizable cluster of *Homo naledi* fossils. At both sites, more fossils remain to be uncovered. The discoveries in the Rising Star caves have changed what we thought we knew of human evolution. And they've raised all kinds of new questions.

Chapter Eighteen

YOU DON'T SAY

A DISCOVERY DOWN THE ROAD

This, our last chapter, is about the possibility of a future discovery. The time is modern day and into the future. The place is somewhere in Mongolia.

This chapter is about the possibility of finding out where a ruler known as Genghis Khan was buried nearly eight hundred years ago.[1] The site of his grave is one of the great unanswered mysteries of archaeology.

Genghis Khan was the ruler of the Mongols—people who lived in what is now Mongolia—in the thirteenth century. The son of a minor chieftain, he came out of nowhere and, in just over

....

1 Khan means "leader." It's actually more accurate to spell his name Chinggis Khan, but since most English-language sources spell it Genghis, we will, too.

twenty years, united nearly all of the nomadic tribes from Central Asia. He went on to rule the largest empire in the history of the world, before or since. The Mongol Empire stretched from Eastern Europe to China.

He died in the year 1227. *How* he died was kept a secret. *Where* he died was also kept a secret. Where he was *buried*? Definitely a secret. According to legend, soldiers traveling with his huge burial procession killed anyone who happened to glimpse the procession as it made its way along the route to the secret burial site. And then the attendants who buried Genghis Khan were also killed. And then the soldiers who'd killed the attendants killed themselves. So no one who knew the location of the grave site remained alive. And therefore no one, to this day, knows where it might be.

One artist's version of what Genghis Khan may have looked like—although it was painted long after his death.

Yet thanks to modern technology, Genghis Khan's long-lost burial site might actually be possible to find.

But we'll get back to this.

WHO WERE THE MONGOLS?

The Mongols were loosely connected tribes of nomadic people who spent much of their lives on horseback, and who grazed their animals according to the seasons. They lived in what is called the Steppe region. These treeless grasslands stretched from Eastern Europe through southern Russia and across Central Asia, interrupted by a few large mountain ranges. It was a horse-centered society. Children were taught to ride before they could walk. A boy's skill in the saddle could determine the path of his career. The best riders became mounted messengers or high-ranking cavalry soldiers.

Mongol girls learned from a young age how to ride and hunt and use a bow and arrow. With men away frequently on military campaigns, girls and women tended flocks, hunted for food, and defended the camps. When not away fighting, Mongol men herded the animals. Every male between the ages of fourteen and sixty could be called up for military duty at any time.

Men shaved their hair short on the tops of their heads and grew it long at the sides. Mongol women usually wore baggy trousers. It was fashionable to pad the hips of their trousers with cotton, and to paint their eyebrows black so that they met in the middle.

HARD BEGINNINGS

Genghis Khan's name at birth was Temüjin, and he was born around 1162. Life on the Steppes was harsh, and Temüjin's child-hood was especially so.

Temüjin's mother, Höelün, had just gotten married when she was kidnapped by a man from a rival tribe. She suddenly found herself married to her kidnapper—who would become Temüjin's father. Her new husband/captor already had at least two sons. After Temüjin, the couple would have three more children.

Temüjin was a timid boy, and often bullied by his older half brother. When Temüjin was about eight, his father died. The cause may or may not have been poison. (It's possible it was just an illness.) The rest of the tribe abandoned the family. Temüjin's mother now had four young children of her own as well as the two other children of her dead husband to look after. The family survived, barely, thanks to Höelün's fierce efforts. She fed the children roots and plants she managed to dig up, and the occasional mice they were able to catch.

Temüjin grew older and became the head of his small clan. He married at nineteen, and slowly won over followers. First individuals, and then whole clans flocked to his side. He earned a reputation for rewarding loyalty and promoting people based on talent, rather than how important their families were.

THE EMPiRE EXPANDS

In 1206, having gained the loyalty of an ever-growing number of tribes and clans and chieftains, Temüjin was proclaimed the leader of the entire Mongol Empire. He took on the title Genghis Khan, which roughly translates as "universal ruler."

Over the next ten years the Mongol armies conquered a huge area of the world. They destroyed dozens of cities and slaughtered millions of people. Yes, millions.

Genghis Khan's soldiers instilled terror wherever they went. His highly disciplined, ruthless army was comprised of excellent horsemen who could ride sixty miles a day. If a ruler surrendered without protest and agreed to pay tribute to the Mongols, his kingdom would usually be spared. Groups that dared to resist were slaughtered. It didn't take long for word to spread throughout the land. The message

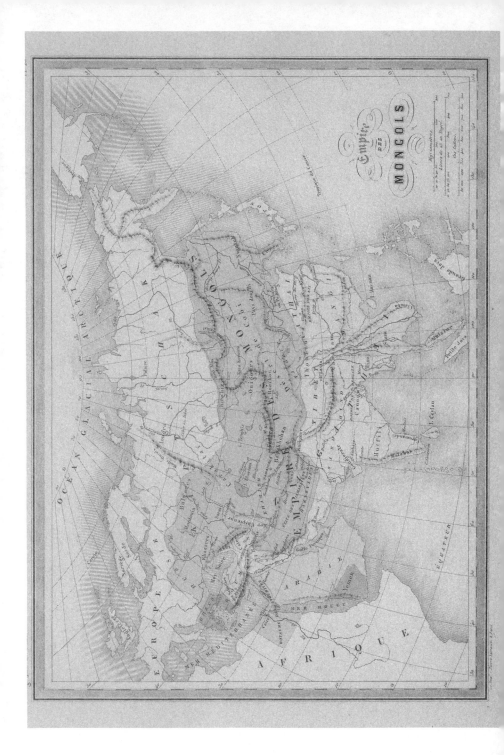

Empire DES MONGOLS

was clear: Surrender and you'll survive. Resist and you will be annihilated.

The Mongols learned and adapted new methods of warfare everywhere they went, often picking up knowledge from people they captured. They learned how to conduct siege warfare from captured Chinese engineers and skilled craftsmen, who were "encouraged" (on pain of death) to share knowledge about gunpowder, catapults, and explosives. Genghis Khan also had the sense to spare bookkeepers and scribes rather than killing them so that they could help with the administration of the empire. Many specialists were forcibly relocated to all corners of the empire so they could help keep it running smoothly.

Mongol soldiers— well trained, disciplined, and ruthless.

BATTLE FROM THE SADDLE

Mongol warriors were highly trained, and their units strictly organized. Genghis Khan's huge armies could travel quickly on the backs of their speedy horses, often surprising their enemies by showing up unexpectedly.

High-ranking soldiers wore armor made of iron pieces sewn to thick leather tunics. Underneath they wore silk undershirts. If an arrow went through their leather or metal outerwear, the silk went into the body with the arrowhead and made it easier to pull the arrow out.

ON THE MONGOL MENU

In peacetime, Mongols ate mutton, beef, and any animals they could catch, including foxes, wolves, rats, and mice. On marches that required traveling long distances speedily, warriors sustained themselves by opening a vein on their horses' necks and drinking the blood. Mounted soldiers and messengers put slabs of raw meat under their saddle. After a day's riding, the "tenderized" meat could be eaten raw. Fermented mare's milk was their alcoholic drink, and Mongols drank a lot of it.

Mongol warriors were famous for firing their arrows at a full gallop, in any direction. Every soldier carried a short bow and both short- and long-range arrows, as well as a sword, an ax, a few javelins (spears), and a dagger. Heavy cavalrymen wore iron helmets and carried a thirteen-foot-long lance fitted with a hook. The hook could yank an enemy soldier out of his saddle, where he wouldn't stand a chance against deadly Mongol swords and battle-axes.

After destroying a city, the Mongols sometimes set the decapitated heads of their victims into concrete to create towers of skulls. The towers served as a grisly reminder to others about what

A Persian painter's portrayal of a battle between the Mongols and the Chinese.

could happen if they were foolish enough to try to resist the Mongols.

THE NOT-SO-GORY DETAILS

From the perspective of the many people who witnessed the terrifying havoc wreaked by thundering armies of Mongol warriors, Genghis Khan was ruthless, violent, and cruel. But to his own people he was considered a wise and fair ruler.

Genghis Khan appreciated talent. Among his high-ranking officers were shepherds, herders, carpenters, and blacksmiths. He spared the lives of captives who could read and write, because he could not. He was also known for his religious tolerance. The Mongols' religion was called shamanism, which combined magic with the worship of gods of nature, as well as an assortment of good and evil spirits. But he permitted people to practice foreign religions, such as Islam and Buddhism.

The Mongols established an extraordinarily successful communication network for the empire. Known as the *yam*, it was a relay system, much like the later US Pony Express. Riders rode tough, sure-footed ponies from one station to the next. The riders ate and slept in the saddle, and covered at least a hundred miles in a day. Rest stations were set up along the route. Riders traveled with bells on so that they could be heard approaching a station, to save time changing ponies and preparing food.

Eventually, the Mongols controlled the entire trade route between China and Europe. Thanks to this network, people in the West learned of cultures they might never have known about and were introduced to things like noodles and tea and playing cards and rice.

THE END

In the second week of August 1227, Genghis Khan was on his way to conquer northern China when he fell ill. Possibly it was typhus. He was probably in his mid-sixties. The ailing Genghis Khan was rushed north in a closed cart to no one knows where. On his deathbed he instructed his sons and attendants to keep his death a secret, so that enemies of the Mongols wouldn't form alliances with one another against the Mongols. He also told them to carry out his plans to annihilate the kingdoms of northern China. So no one spilled the beans that he was dead.

If we're to believe historians who lived about a century after

Genghis Khan's death, the Khan's corpse was brought in a long procession across the Gobi Desert and all the way to the homeland of the Mongols, where it was buried in a secret grave. Such a trip would have taken a minimum of three weeks, and it was the height of summer.

Parts of this story don't add up. As one modern historian points out, if you're trying to keep the great Khan's death a secret, why broadcast it with a huge procession, carrying an increasingly stinky dead body several hundred miles? And why kill anyone who happens to be nearby when the procession passes, leaving a long trail of slain victims in your path? If you think about it, a trail of dead bodies is the thirteenth-century equivalent of a large blinking neon arrow. So the killing-everyone-related-to-the-burial theory

Hollywood has made quite a few extremely inauthentic movies about Genghis Khan's life.

seems . . . unlikely. What seems more likely is that a small group quickly and stealthily brought the body somewhere to be buried.

But where?

BACK TO THE PRESENT

Lots of people want to find Genghis Khan's burial place. Many modern-day Mongolians would like to honor and celebrate the site. Archaeologists could learn a great deal of history if they located the tomb and studied its contents.

But there's a hitch: First, there might not even *be* a tomb. There's a chance his body was cremated. Or that it was left on the side of a mountain, in the shamanist religious tradition. And even if there *is* a hidden tomb somewhere, many people in modern-day Mongolia consider it a sacred place and want it left alone. In modern-day Mongolia, Genghis Khan is revered as a national hero. Streets, children, and candy bars are named after him. His face appears on stamps, buildings, and Mongolian money. Mongolians don't want foreign treasure hunters and archaeologists digging around their sacred places.

Here's where a modern technology called ultra-high-resolution satellite imaging can help. In 2005 researchers at the University of California at San Diego, in partnership with National Geographic, put together a landscape they called a "virtual exploration system." They invited ordinary people to tag anomalies in the vast Mongolian landscape and to note anything that might be a promising place to look. As many as ten thousand volunteer participants have helped look for the tomb of Genghis Khan, using their own computers. They haven't located anything yet, but they've tagged a lot of anomalies for investigation.

This technology may help locate a lot of other archaeological sites around the world, as yet undiscovered. It can harness the observational power of millions of amateur archaeologists. And you could be one of them.

A LiTTLE MORE DiRT
ON ARCHAEOLOGY

HOW ARCHAEOLOGISTS DATE ARTIFACTS

How do archaeologists know how old something is? Here are some techniques they use.

🔍 **Context:** They pay attention to what's near an object or artifact. They examine the soil or rock that it was found in. Stuff like ancient plants, animals, and even grains of pollen can help date something. That's why mapping and documenting are such important parts of the archaeological process.

🔍 **Radiometric dating:** Archaeologists use this technique to measure the amount of radioactive elements in an object to see when a rock was formed or when an animal or plant died. Carbon dating is one form of radiometric dating. All living things absorb carbon from the atmosphere. When a plant or animal dies, it stops taking in any carbon. And because some forms of carbon are radioactive, they break down at a set rate over a specific period of time. This rate is known as a half-life. Measuring the half-life of the radioactive form of carbon (called C-14) helps archaeologists determine the age of once-living materials like wood, textile, food, and bones.

Q Stratigraphy: Over time layers of soil and sediments (strata) build up. Stratigraphy is the study of those layers. Unless an area has been disturbed, the deeper you go, the older the layers are. So older artifacts tend to be found in deeper strata and newer ones tend to be closer to the surface.

Q Thermoluminescence dating: Archaeologists use this technique to date objects like volcanic rock, flint tools, or clay that was fired in a kiln. These objects contain minerals that have absorbed and trapped certain electrons. Upon being heated, or even exposed to sunlight, the objects have released these trapped electrons at a known rate. Archaeologists can use thermoluminescence dating to measure how much time has passed since the object was last heated to a high temperature. It's useful for dating things like pottery, terra-cotta warriors, or the layers of pyroclastic sediment that buried the town of Herculaneum.

DiG THIS

You've probably noticed that the field of archaeology has come a long way. In earlier times, white European "archaeologists"[1]

....
1   But actually more like tomb raiders or treasure hunters.

traveled to promising places, dug up artifacts and treasures, and then shipped home whatever they thought was of value.

In the United States, white treasure hunters and early archaeologists collected Indigenous peoples' cultural artifacts, dug up their burial grounds, and removed human remains and sacred items. They sold them for profit, or shipped them off to museums for scientific study.

It's no longer acceptable to dig up and carry away the stones, bones, and artifacts that belong to another country or culture.

Today legitimate archaeologists follow strict legal and ethical guidelines. They obtain permission before they excavate a site. They don't keep, sell, or trade the artifacts that they uncover.

Modern archaeologists carefully survey, record, and document the location and surrounding of each artifact they find before they remove it. And then they analyze and publish their findings so that others can conduct further studies.

WHO OWNS THE STONES AND BONES?

Nowadays many countries have passed laws that prohibit artifacts and human remains from leaving the country where they were found. Increasing numbers of museums have honored the wishes of Indigenous peoples (Native American, First Nation, and Indigenous people of Australia, for instance) and returned artifacts and human remains to their communities for proper reburial. In the US, a 1990 law called the Native American Graves Protection and Repatriation Act requires federal agencies and museums to take an inventory of their collections. They must open discussions and, if requested, return certain cultural artifacts to representatives of the tribal communities from which they were taken or bought or—more often than not—stolen. The law also protects Indigenous burial sites and grants Indigenous communities the right to grant permission for excavation on protected lands. Nowadays it's a federal crime in the US to sell or even possess many cultural artifacts.

Still, conflicts continue to flare up between archaeologists interested in studying artifacts for their historical significance and Indigenous communities that wish for the return and reburial of remains and objects belonging to their ancestral heritage. Luckily, this complex issue can sometimes be avoided, thanks to modern technology. Rather than barging around protected or sacred places, archaeologists can gather data remotely, through a technique called geophysical surveying. This technology can include aerial photography, drone footage, radar and sonar sensing, airborne laser scanning, and satellite images. Even kids can learn to use some of it. (See page 184-5.)

It's no wonder many Indigenous people remain wary toward people wishing to study their cultural artifacts. While archaeologists like to think of their work as purely scientific—based on concrete evidence that's been dug up, evaluated, and scientifically verified—the fact is that everyone is a product of their own cultural background, as we've seen many times in this book. Many conclusions about human history based on archaeological evidence that were once considered to be widely accepted facts are now being reevaluated. It's important to continue to question our own cultural biases and how they might affect the way we interpret the past.

HOW TO BE AN AMATEUR ARCHAEOLOGIST: EXPECT THE UNEXPECTED

1. Keep your eyes open. Look for anomalies and keyholes in the landscape.

2. If you locate something, don't touch it. Record its location as best as you can. Take a picture if you can. Once an artifact is removed from its setting, it becomes less valuable as a source of information for scientists.

3. If you locate something, ask a grown-up to help you find an archaeologist. In the US, each state has an office of historical preservation (ncshpo.org) or a state archaeologist. You can also contact your local museum, historical society, or university.

4. In most areas of the world, you need permission to dig for artifacts. It's almost always against the law to remove artifacts from public lands and take them home. If you find something small, like a coin, or an arrowhead, or if it's something found in a place that you can't record with accuracy, such as a 1,500-year-old sword at the bottom of a lake, remove it carefully, note the location as best you can, and then go back to step 3.

AUTHOR'S NOTE

The chance discoveries I wrote about in this book are just some of the amazing stories I unearthed in my research. There are many, many more discoveries that have transformed our understanding of the past. Practically every week, there's another news story.

Take these, for instance:

Q A man in Turkey who was renovating his home in 1963 knocked down a wall and discovered an ancient underground city.

Q In South Africa in 2008, a nine-year-old boy found a fossil that turned out to belong to a previously unknown hominid species that lived almost two million years ago.

Q At the site of New York's World Trade Center in 2010, workers discovered the remains of an eighteenth-century ship.

Q In 2018 an eight-year-old girl fished a sword out of a lake in Sweden. It turned out to be 1,500 years old.

Q During sewer construction in London in 2018, workers found the five-hundred-year-old body of a man. He was still wearing thigh-high boots.

You see what I mean? There's still so much more to learn about our past. New discoveries happen all the time, and sometimes what's uncovered can cause us to question much of what we thought we knew.

If you've made it all the way through this book, then maybe you have dreams of becoming an archaeologist when you grow up. In the meantime, you can try to become an accidental archaeologist yourself (see page 191 on how to start), or you can find more amazing stories of accidental discoveries and write about them. Archaeology is awesome. The opportunities are endless.

SELECTED BIBLIOGRAPHY

"The Antikythera Mechanism Research Project." http://www.antikythera-mechanism.gr/.

Asingh, Pauline, and Niels Lynnerup, eds. *Grauballe Man: An Iron Age Bog Body Revisited*. Moesgård: Jutland Archaeological Society, 2007.

Beard, Mary. "When Did Vesuvius Erupt?" *Times Literary Supplement*, October 22, 2018.

Beckham, Mike, writer, producer, director. *The 2000-Year-Old Computer—Decoding the Antikythera Mechanism*. BBC Documentary video. MMXII Images First Ltd. Video available online.

Belzoni, Giovanni Battista. "Narrative of the Operations and Recent Discoveries within the Pyramids, Temples, Tombs, and Excavations, in Egypt and Nubia; and of a Journey to the Coast of the Red Sea, in Search of the Ancient Berenice; and Another to the Oasis of Jupiter Ammon." Originally published London: John Murray, 1820. New York: Scribner, Welford, and Armstrong, 1970.

Bennett, Amanda. "Wanted: Fit, Fearless Scientist for Huge Underground Find." *National Geographic*, September 17, 2015.

Berger, Lee R., and John Hawks. *Almost Human: The Astonishing Tale of Homo Naledi and the Discovery That Changed Our Human Story*. Washington, DC: National Geographic Partners, 2017.

Berger, Lee R., John Hawks, Darryl J. de Ruiter, et al . "*Homo Naledi*, a New Species of the Genus *Homo* from the Dinaledi Chamber, South Africa." *eLIFE*, September 1, 2015.

Bernard, H. Russell. "Kalymnian Sponge Diving." *Human Biology* 39, no. 2 (May 1967): 103–130.

Blaxland, Beth. "Hominid and Hominin—What's the Difference?" *Australian Museum*, February 11, 2018.

Cantwell, Anne-Marie E., and Diana diZerega Wall. *Unearthing Gotham: The Archaeology of New York City*. New Haven: Yale University Press, 2003.

Cavendish, Richard. "Discovery of the Lascaux Cave Paintings." *History Today*, September 9, 2015.

Clynes, Tom. "Watch: How to Become a Space Archaeologist." *National Geographic*, January 30, 2017.

Cockle, W. E. H. "Restoring and Conserving Papyri." *Bulletin of the Institute of Classical Studies* 30 (1983): 147-65.

Cotterell, Arthur. *The First Emperor of China: The Greatest Archeological Find of Our Time*. New York: Holt, Rinehart and Winston, 1981.

Countryman, Edward. *Enjoy the Same Liberty: Black Americans and the Revolutionary Era*. Lanham, MD: Rowman & Littlefield, 2014.

de Solla Price, Derek. "Antikythera Mechanism." http://derekdesollaprice.org/antikythera-mechanism/.

Jacques Cousteau Odyssey: Diving for Roman Plunder. Documentary, 1980. Video available online.

Cullen, Bob. "Testimony from the Iceman." *Smithsonian* magazine, February 2003.

Cuvigny, Helene, and Adam Bulow-Jacobsen. "The Finds of Papyri: The Archaeology of Papyrology." In *The Oxford Handbook of Papyrology*, 30–58, edited by Roger S. Bagnall. New York: Oxford University Press, 2012.

David, Ariel. "Archaeologists Find the Last Hideout of the Jewish Revolt in Jerusalem." *Haaretz*, May 10, 2016.

Davison, Michael Worth, and Neal V. Martin, eds. *Everyday Life through the Ages*. London: Reader's Digest, 1992.

Davoli, Paola. "Papyri, Archaeology, and Modern History: A Contextual Study of the Beginnings of Papyrology and Egyptology." *Bulletin of the American Society of Papyrologists* 52 (2015): 87–112.

Dawn of Humanity. Video. Produced by NOVA and National Geographic Studios for WGBH Boston, 2015. Video available online.

Deiss, Joseph Jay. *Herculaneum: Italy's Buried Treasure*. J. Paul Getty Museum, 1989.

Dell'Amore, Christine. "Who Were the Ancient Bog Mummies? Surprising New Clues." *National Geographic*, July 18, 2014.

Denoble, Petar. "The Story of Sponge Divers." Alert Diver Online, 2011.

Dirks, Paul H. G. M., Eric M. Roberts, Hannah Hilbert-Wolf, et al. "The Age of *Homo Naledi* and Associated Sediments in the Rising Star Cave, South Africa." *eLIFE*, May 9, 2017.

"The Discovery of Tollund Man." Museum Silkeborg. http://www.museumsilkeborg.dk/the-discovery-of-tollund-man.

Draper, Robert. "Unburying the Aztec." *National Geographic*, November 2010.

Drewett, Peter. *Field Archaeology: An Introduction*. London: UCL Press, 1999.

Dunmore's Proclamation, November 11, 1775. https://www.loc.gov/resource/rbpe.1780180b/

Eshleman, Clayton. "Lectures on the Ice-Age Painted Caves of Southwestern France." *Interval(le)s* 11.2–111.1 (Fall 2008/Winter 2009) 235–70.

Fagan, Brian M. *The Rape of the Nile: Tomb Robbers, Tourists, and Archaeologists in Egypt*. Boulder, CO: Westview Press, 2004.

Foley, Brendan. "The Antikythera Shipwreck: Excavating the World's Richest Ancient Shipwreck." Video of lecture available online.

Franklin, Benjamin. "Felons and Rattlesnakes, 9 May 1751." *Founders Online*, National Archives and Records Administration.

Frazier, Ian. "Invaders." *New Yorker*, June 19, 2017.

Freedman, Russell. *In the Days of the Vaqueros: America's First True Cowboys.* New York: Clarion Books, 2001.

Freeth, Tony. "Decoding an Ancient Computer." *Scientific American* 301, no. 6 (December 2009): 76–83.

Gandy, S. Kay. "Legacy of the American West: Indian Cowboys, Black Cowboys, and Vaqueros." *Social Education* 72, no. 4 (May/June 2008): 189–93.

Glob, P. V. *The Bog People: Iron-Age Man Preserved.* Translated from the Danish by Rupert Bruce-Mitford. New York: Faber and Faber, 1969.

Goodman, A. H., J. Jones, J. Reid, et al. "Isotopic and Elemental Chemistry of Teeth: Implications for Places of Birth, Forced Migration Patterns, Nutritional Status, and Pollution." W. Montague Cobb Research Laboratory.

Grenfell, Bernard P., Arthur S. Hunt, and J. Gilbart Smyly, eds. *The Tebtunis Papyri.* London: Henry Frowde, Oxford University Press, 1902.

Greshko, Michael. "Did This Mysterious Ape-Human Once Live Alongside Our Ancestors?" *National Geographic*, May 9, 2017.

"2012 Grey Friars Excavation." Richard III – Archaeological dig. University of Leicester. https://www.le.ac.uk/richardiii/archaeology/wherewedug.html.

Hansen, Joyce, and Gary McGowan. *Breaking Ground, Breaking Silence: The Story of New York's African Burial Ground.* New York: Henry Holt, 1998.

Hart, Edward, director. *Ghosts of Murdered Kings: Bronze Age Bog Bodies Reveal the Strange Beliefs of the Long-Vanished Peoples of Europe.* NOVA: PBS, 2013. Video available online.

Hawks, John, Marina Elliott, Peter Schmid, et al. "New Fossil Remains of *Homo Naledi* from the Lesedi Chamber, South Africa." *eLIFE*, May 9, 2017.

Hawks, John. "Renewed Excavations in the Rising Star Cave." *Medium*, September 11, 2017.

Heeres, J. E. *The Part Borne by the Dutch in the Discovery of Australia 1606–1765.* London: Royal Dutch Geographical Society, 1899.

Hendry, Lisa. "*Homo Naledi*, Your Most Recently Discovered Human Relative." *Natural History Museum* (London) magazine, September 2018.

"Herculaneum, Saving the Site." *World Archaeology*, September 19, 2018.

"How 900-Year-Old African Coins Found in Australia May Finally Solve the Mystery of Who Arrived Down Under First." *Daily Mail* Online, August 22, 2013.

"How Ancient Papyrus Was Made." Papyrology Collection. University of Michigan Library. March 11, 2014.

Hume, Ivor Noël. *Belzoni: The Giant Archaeologists Love to Hate.* Charlottesville: University of Virginia Press, 2011.

Ilany, Ofri. "Scholar: The Essenes, Dead Sea Scroll 'Authors,' Never Existed." *Haaretz*, March 13, 2009.

Keys, David, and Nicholas Pyke. "Decoded at Last: The 'Classical Holy Grail' That May Rewrite the History of the World." *Independent*, April 17, 2005.

——————. "Eureka! Extraordinary Discovery Unlocks Secrets of the Ancients." *Independent*, April 17, 2005.

King, Turi E., Gloria Gonzalez Fortes, Patricia Balaresque, et al. "Identification of the Remains of King Richard III." *Nature Communications*, December 2, 2014.

Knapton, Ernest John. *Empress Josephine*. Cambridge: Harvard University Press, 1963.

Koch, Peter O. *The Aztecs, the Conquistadors, and the Making of Mexican Culture*. Jefferson, NC: McFarland, 2006.

Lane, George. *Genghis Khan and Mongol Rule*. Indianapolis: Hackett, 2009.

"Lascaux Cave Paintings: Layout, Meaning, Photographs of Prehistoric Animal Pictures." *Stone Age Art* in *Art Encyclopedia* online.

Lawler, Andrew. "Who Wrote the Dead Sea Scrolls?" *Smithsonian* magazine, January 1, 2010.

Lennon, Troy. "How a Dog Called Robot Helped Reveal Lascaux's Prehistoric Art Gallery." *Daily Telegraph*, September 10, 2015.

Lewis, Danny. "Skeleton Pulled from the Antikythera Shipwreck Could Give Clues to Life Aboard the Vessel." *Smithsonian* magazine, September 20, 2016.

Lin, Albert Yu-Min, Andrew Huynh, Gert Lanckriet, and Luke Barrington. "Crowdsourcing the Unknown: The Satellite Search for Genghis Khan." *PLOS ONE*, December 30, 2014.

Loewen, James K. *Lies My Teacher Told Me*. New York: Touchstone, 2007.

Macintyre, Ben. "We Know Oetzi Had Fleas, His Last Supper Was Steak . . . and He Died 5,300 Years Ago." *Times* (London), November 1, 2003.

Maehler, H. A New Method of Dismounting Papyrus Cartonnage. *Bulletin of the Institute of Classical Studies* 27 (1980): 120–22.

Magness, Jodi. "What's the Poop on Ancient Toilets and Toilet Habits?" *Near Eastern Archaeology* 75, no. 2 (2012): 80–87.

Man, John. *The Terracotta Army: China's First Emperor and the Birth of a Nation*. Boston: Da Capo Press, 2008.

Mancini, Mark. "Peat Bogs Are Freakishly Good at Preserving Human Remains." HowStuffWorks, January 23, 2019.

Marchant, Jo. "The World's First Computer May Have Been Used to Tell Fortunes." *Smithsonian* magazine, June 8, 2016.

McCauley, Brea, David Maxwell, and Mark Collard. "A Cross-Cultural Perspective on Upper Palaeolithic Hand Images with Missing Phalanges." *Journal of Paleolithic Archaeology* 1, no. 4 (December 2018): 314–33.

McCoy, Terrence. "The Frustrating Hunt for Genghis Khan's Long-Lost Tomb Just Got a Whole Lot Easier." *Washington Post*, January 8, 2015.

McIntosh, Ian S. "Life and Death on the Wessel Islands: The Case of Australia's Mysterious African Coin Cache." *Australian Folklore* 27 (November 2012): 9–29.

Medford, Edna Greene, Emilyn L. Brown, Linda Heywood, and John Thornton. "Slavery and Freedom in New Amsterdam." In *Historical Perspectives of the African Burial Ground: New York Blacks and the Diaspora*, edited by Edna Greene Medford. Vol. 3 of *The New York African Burial Ground: Unearthing the African Presence in Colonial New York*. Washington, DC: Howard University Press, 2009.

Medford, Edna Greene, Emilyn L. Brown, and Selwyn H. H. Carrington. "Change and Adjustment." In *Historical Perspectives of the African Burial Ground: New York Blacks and the Diaspora*, edited by Edna Greene Medford. Vol. 3 of *The New York African Burial Ground: Unearthing the African Presence in Colonial New York*. Washington DC: Howard University Press, 2009.

Meltzer, David J., Lawrence C. Todd, and Vance T. Holliday. "The Folsom (Paleoindian) Type Site: Past Investigations, Current Studies." *American Antiquity* 67, no. 1 (2002): 5.

Mendelsohn, Daniel. "Girl, Interrupted: Who Was Sappho?" *New Yorker*, March 9, 2015.

_____. "Hearing Sappho." *New Yorker*, March 12, 2015.

Minor, Sarah. "Handling the Beast." *Conjunctions* 61 (2013): 18–26.

Mishra, Patit Paban. *The History of Thailand*. Santa Barbara: Greenwood, 2010.

Moctezuma, Eduardo Matos, and David Hiser. "New Finds in the Great Temple." *National Geographic*, December 1980.

"Myths and Legends." University of Leicester, Richard III project site.

Obbink, Dirk. "Ten Poems of Sappho: Provenance, Authenticity, and Text of the New Sappho Papyri." In *The Newest Sappho: P. Sapph. Obbink and P. GC Inv. 105, Frs 1-4*, edited by Anton Bierl and André Lardinois, 34–54. Vol. 2 of *Studies in Archaic and Classical Greek Song*.

Owen, James. "5 Surprising Facts about Ötzi the Iceman." *National Geographic*, March 20, 2015.

Oxyrhynchus: A City and Its Texts. Online exhibition. Accessed April 25, 2019. http://www.papyrology.ox.ac.uk/POxy/VExhibition/exhib_welcome.html.

Parpola, Simo. *Letters from Assyrian Scholars to the Kings Esarhaddon and Assurbanipal.* Winona Lake, IN: Eisenbrauns, 2007.

Parry, J. "Giovani Baptista Belzoni." An 1804 broadside, now in the British Museum. https://www.britishmuseum.org/.

Parry, Simon. "Curse of the Warriors." *South China Morning Post*, September 14, 2007.

Parsons, P. J. "Waste Paper City." Oxyrhynchus: A City and Its Texts. Online exhibition. http://www.papyrology.ox.ac.uk/POxy/oxyrhynchus/parsons1.html.

Pfeiffer, Leslie. "The Folsom Culture." *Central States Archaeological Journal* 51, no. 4: 50th Anniversary Issue! (October 1, 2004): 173–75.

Pitts, Michael W. *Digging for Richard III: The Search for the Lost King*. New York: Thames & Hudson, 2014.

Pliny the Younger. *Letters*, Book 6, translated by J. B. Firth, 1900. http://www.attalus.org/old/pliny6.html.

Plutarch. *Lives*. Translated by Bernadotte Perrin. Vol. 9 in Loeb Classical Library, 1920.

Pocha, Jehangir S. "Mongolia Sees Genghis Khan's Good Side." *New York Times*, May 10, 2005.

Pompeii: Life and Death with Mary Beard. Timeline documentary of ancient Rome (originally BBC), 2015. Video available online.

Pra Buddha Mahasuwan Patimakorn (Golden Buddha). An online history of the Golden Buddha. gba.orgfree.com/history%20of%20golden%20buddha.html.

Preston, Douglas. "Fossils & the Folsom Cowboy." *Natural History* 106, no. 1 (February 1997): 16–21.

Quarles, Benjamin, Thad W. Tate, and Gary Nash. *The Negro in the American Revolution*. Chapel Hill: University of North Carolina Press, 1961.

Ramirez, Janina. *The Cave Art Paintings of the Lascaux Cave—with Professor Alice Roberts*. Video, February 8, 2017. https://play.acast.com/s/artdetective/thecaveartpaintingsofthelascauxcave-withprofessoraliceroberts.

Richmond, Ben. "Finding Genghis Khan's Tomb from Space." VICE, "Motherboard," January 5, 2015.

Roaf, Michael. "Mesopotamian Kings and the Built Environment." In *Experiencing Power, Generating Authority: Cosmos, Politics, and the Ideology of Kingship in Ancient Egypt and Mesopotamia*, edited by Jane A. Hill, Philip Jones, and Antonio J. Morales, 331–60. Philadelphia: University of Pennsylvania Museum of Archaeology and Anthropology, 2013.

Rodriguez, Carmela. "Richard III Had Lavish Diet of Swan and Wine, New Forensic Study Reveals." *History Extra*, January 18, 2018.

Rojas, José Luis de. *Tenochtitlan: Capital of the Aztec Empire*. Gainseville: University Press of Florida, 2012.

"The Romans Destroy the Temple at Jerusalem, 70 AD." EyeWitness to History, 2005.

Rothstein, Edward. "A Burial Ground and Its Dead Are Given Life." *New York Times*, February 25, 2010.

Ruspoli, Mario. *The Cave of Lascaux: The Final Photographs*. New York: Abrams, 1987.

Ryan, Donald P. "BA Portrait: Giovanni Battista Belzoni." *Biblical Archaeologist* 49, no. 3 (1986): 133–38.

Schlissel, Lillian. *Black Frontiers: A History of African American Heroes in the Old West*. New York: Simon & Schuster Books for Young Readers, 1995.

Schmidt-Chevalier, Michel. "Were the Cave Paintings in Southwest France Made by Women?" *Leonardo* 14, no. 4 (1981): 302–303.

Schoonover, Mike. "Folsom Man Archaeological Site." Folsom Village. Essay, November 27, 2010. http://www.folsomvillage.com/FolsomManSite.html.

Seabrook, John. "The Invisible Library." *New Yorker*, November 16, 2015.

Shakespeare, *Richard III*. http://shakespeare.mit.edu/richardiii/full.html.

Sharpe, Emily. "Armchair Archaeologists Reveal Details of Life in Ancient Egypt." Archaeology and Conservation WordPress, February 29, 2016.

Shreeve, Jamie. "This Face Changes the Human Story. But How?" *National Geographic*, September 10, 2015.

Sider, David. *The Library of the Villa Dei Papiri at Herculaneum*. J. Paul Getty Museum, 2005.

Sigurdsson, Haraldur, et al. "The Dead Do Tell Tales at Vesuvius." *National Geographic*, May 1984, 557–613.

Smith, Ronald Bishop. *Siam; or, The History of the Thais*. Bethesda, MD: Decatur Press, 1966.

Sutton, John Edward Giles. *A Thousand Years of East Africa*. Nairobi, Kenya: British Institute in Eastern Africa, 1992.

Tacitus, Cornelius. *Germania*. AD 98.

Than, Ker. "Dead Sea Scrolls Mystery Solved?" *National Geographic*, July 27, 2010.

Thomas, David Hurst. *Skull Wars: Kennewick Man, Archaeology, and the Battle for Native American Identity*. New York: Basic Books, 2000.

Thomas, Robert McG., Jr. "Marcel Ravidat Is Dead at 72; Found Lascaux Cave Paintings." *New York Times*, March 31, 1995.

Urbanus, Jason. "The Race to Crack the Code." *Archaeology* magazine, November/December 2017.

Weiss, Daniel. "Scroll Search." *Archaeology* magazine, May/June2017.

Wilson, Cameron. "1000-Year-Old Coin Discovery in the Top End." Radio National (Australia), May 30, 2013.

Wong, Kate. "Mystery Human." *Scientific American* 314, no. 3 (2016): 28–37.

_____. "Our Cousin Neo." *Scientific American* 317, no. 2 (Aug. 2017): 46–47.

Wyatt, David K. *Thailand: A Short History*. New Haven: Yale University Press, 2003.

Zimmer, Carl. "How Did We Get to Be Human?" *New York Times*, November 19, 2018.

SOURCE NOTES

Introduction: A Bunch of Amateurs
p. vii: One archaeologist calls . . . "keyholes": Drewett, 57.
Chapter One: A Blast from the Past
p. 2: Workers . . . Spanish king's treasury: Deiss, 35.
p. 4: The ball, called a *pila* . . . bladders: Deiss, 134.
p. 4: giant column . . . mushroom-shaped cloud: Deiss, 4.
p. 4: "cloud of unusual size and appearance": Pliny, 16.
p. 8: The massive surge . . . the flow: Sigurdsson, 576.
p. 9: "blacker and denser than any ordinary night": Pliny, 16.
p. 9: "Broad sheets of fire . . . fearful black cloud": ibid.
p. 9: "Many besought . . . for evermore": ibid.
p. 9: "everything changed . . . like snowdrifts": ibid.
pp. 9–10: For a long time . . . embrace: *Pompeii: Life and Death with Mary Beard*.
pp. 10–11: Excavation continues . . . beams: "Herculaneum, Saving the Site."
p. 11: "Of course . . . for history": Pliny, 16.
p. 6 [sidebar]: But recent . . . in October: Beard, "When Did Vesuvius Erupt?"
Chapter Two: Etched in Stone
p. 13: one valuable . . . hunk of rock: Fagan, 50.
p. 15: He'd been writing . . . his esteem: Knapton, 298.
p. 16: pencils . . . lead bullets: Fagan, 50.
p. 17: The British scholar . . . people's names: Urbanus.
p. 18: "I've got it!": Champollion as quoted in Urbanus.
Chapter Three: A Giant in the Field
p. 20: As he struts . . . collective breath: Hume, p. 28.
pp. 20–22: "He clasps round . . . on the rope": J. Parry.
p. 22: His father . . . grandchildren: Belzoni, 20.
pp. 22–23: When Giovanni was sixteen . . . Great Belzoni: Fagan, 66–67.
p. 23: He also met . . . Sarah Barre: Hume, 15.
p. 23: During that time . . . large loads: Belzoni, 69.
p. 26: Belzoni once got . . . his guides: Hume, 31.
p. 31: Belzoni enjoyed . . . forty-five years old: Fagan, 148.
Chapter Four: In a Pile, Crocodile
pp. 34–35: Suddenly the man spots . . . been stuffed with . . . papyrus: Grenfell, Hunt, and Smyly, vi.
p. 36: "town of the sharp-snouted fish": Parsons.
p. 37: such as ancient tax . . . and horoscopes: Sharpe.
pp. 37–38: To make papyrus . . . one hundred feet: "How Ancient Papyrus Was Made"; Cockle, 147.
p. 38: To produce . . . out loud: Sider, 29.
p. 39: Papyrus wasn't very durable . . . reused: Obbink, 34.
p. 39: Or it might . . . sarcophagus: Cockle, 150.
p. 39: Some methods . . . than others: Cockle, 156–58.

p. 41: Thanks to new . . . infrared lighting: Maehler, 120–22.

p. 42: Papyrologists expect . . . Sappho: Keys and Pyke, "Eureka!"

p. 36 [sidebar]: That explains why papyri . . . early Persian: Keys and Pyke, "Decoded at Last."

Chapter Five: What a Wreck

pp. 43–44, 47: The year is 1900 . . . ancient shipwreck: For an account of the discovery, see *Jacques Cousteau Odyssey*.

pp. 48–49: Those of one . . . married in Rome: Foley.

p. 49: A few years later . . . curious object: de Solla Price.

p. 50: In fact . . . *was* a computer: "Antikythera Mechanism Research Project."

p. 52: Could he have built it? : Freeth, 83.

p. 52: In 2016 . . . looked like: Lewis.

pp. 45–46 [sidebar]: Diving Difficulties . . . many a young man: For the history of Greek sponge diving, see Bernard, 103–30, and Denoble.

p. 51 [sidebar]: Astronomers and . . . his throne, unharmed: Beckham; Parpola, xxiv.

p. 51 [footnote]: In one case . . . remain king: Roaf, 334.

Chapter Six: Proving a Point

pp. 53–54: As George approaches . . . lot of them: Meltzer, Todd, and Holliday, 7.

p. 57: His father . . . now free: Preston.

p. 58: His integrity . . . boundaries: ibid.

p. 58: But his real love . . . telescope: ibid.

p. 60: And then, in 1927 . . . one of the bison: Meltzer, Todd, and Holliday, 8; Schoonover.

p. 60: That was proof . . . ten thousand years ago: Pfeiffer, 173.

p. 61: Their creation stories . . . to the south: D. Thomas, 164–65.

p. 61: Discoveries such as George McJunkin's . . . came from: D. Thomas, 207.

pp. 61–62: George McJunkin received . . . Black man: Meltzer, Todd, and Holliday, 7.

p. 56 [sidebar]: By the late 1600s . . . the Spanish: Freedman, 6.

p. 56 [sidebar]: The earliest American cowboys learned . . . the vaqueros: Freedman, 50; Gandy.

p. 56 [sidebar]: In the later nineteenth . . . of every four cowboys was black: Schlissel, 30.

Chapter Seven: Paleo Painters

pp. 63–64: One day in early September . . . Robot: Minor, 22.

pp. 64–65: They notify . . . prehistory society: Cavendish.

p. 65: "Once I arrived . . . my eyes": Ruspoli, 189.

p. 66: It isn't until after . . . discovery: R. Thomas; Lennon.

p. 66: The creators . . . France today: Ruspoli, 17.

p. 67: The Magdalenians painted images . . . tent coverings: Eshleman.

p. 68: Some archaeologists . . . than just gathering: Schmidt-Chevalier, 302.

p. 69: Some of the handprints . . . frostbite: McCauley, Maxwell, and Collard, 323; "Lascaux Cave Paintings."

p. 69: They probably applied . . . vegetable fiber: Ruspoli, 194.

Chapter Eight: The Case of the Copper Coins

p. 71: The year is 1944 . . . on the beach: McIntosh, 9.

p. 71: Maurie is . . . now-deserted chain: McIntosh, 23.

p. 72: The upshot . . . of Africa: McIntosh, 11–13.

p. 74: The foreigner was . . . the "Wesel" Islands: McIntosh, 10.

p. 75: "sandal-wood, nutmegs, cloves or other spices": Heeres, 21.

p. 75: "let fly their . . . shouts": Heeres, 30.

p. 76: "these Thieves and Villains introduc'd among us": Franklin.

pp. 77–78: Ships from Kilwa . . . imperial court: Sutton, p. 69.

p. 78: At the time . . . Persian Gulf: "900-Year-Old African Coins."

p. 80: According to Yolngu . . . in China: McIntosh, 14.

p. 80: Yolngu people . . . in the area: McIntosh, 16.

p. 81: Maybe a Dutch vessel was shipwrecked: McIntosh, 17.

p. 81: Recently . . . Cook's arrival: "900-Year-Old African Coins."

Chapter Nine: Scroll Up

p. 82: a donkey ride . . . Jericho: Lawler.

p. 85: The scrolls date . . . Commandments: Lawler.

p. 86: "Miscellaneous Items for Sale . . . or group": *Wall Street Journal*, June 1, 1954.

pp. 86–87: We know about . . . Josephus: As quoted in "Romans Destroy the Temple."

p. 87: The Essenes were . . . Sabbath: Magness, 82–83.

p. 87: But there are scholars . . . stuff up: Ilany.

p. 87: It may have been . . . tannery: Lawler.

p. 88: What happened next . . . scholars: For a good overview of different theories about who wrote them and who hid them, see David; Lawler; or Than.

p. 88: They fled . . . sewers: David.

p. 88: and then hurriedly . . . Roman army: Lawler.

p. 88: In 2017 . . . caves in the area: Weiss.

Chapter Ten: Bogged Down

p. 89: "There's something strange here": "Discovery of Tollund Man."

p. 91: But when the police learn . . . archaeologists: ibid.

p. 93: Today they're . . . Denmark: Dell'Amore; Hart.

p. 93: Tollund Man . . . 375 BCE: Asingh and Lynnerup, 294.

p. 94: Both Tollund Man . . . other weeds: Glob, 33.

p. 95: Sometimes, the Cimbri . . . at the shoulders: Tacitus.

p. 95: "twisting their hair and pulling it up in a knot": ibid.

p. 95: "all this elaborate make-up . . . meet in battle": ibid.

p. 95: "They endured . . . the summits": Plutarch (23:1) 525.

p. 96: It dates to . . . blood collected: "Discovery of Tollund Man."

pp. 97–98: Other historians suggest . . . successful harvest: Hart.

p. 94 [sidebar]: The sphagnum also dissolves . . . pickled organs: Mancini.

Chapter Eleven: Lucky Break

pp. 99–100: For twenty years . . . is pure gold: Pra Buddha Mahasuwan Patimakorn.

p. 104: He ranks . . . Thai alphabet: Smith, 33.

p. 104: "great" and "beautiful" . . . "18 cubits high": Smith, 101.

p. 107: More than 100,000 . . . or Paris: Smith, 75.

p. 107: "the dust beneath your majesty's feet": Britannica Academic, "Thailand."

p. 107: "introducing love poems in the palace": Smith, 57.

p. 108: An army of 1.5 million . . . Ayutthaya: Mishra, 65.

p. 108: One of the most . . . to ashes: Mishra, 65.

p. 108: Concerned courtiers . . . sandalwood club: Wyatt, 128.

Chapter Twelve: Eternally Yours

p. 110: The Yang brothers' . . . Mount Li: S. Parry.

p. 114: The First Emperor . . . eye on them: Man, 75.

p. 116: "The First Emperor . . . be divided": Cotterell, 157.

p. 117: To disguise the stench . . . the capital: ibid.

Chapter Thirteen: Temple of Gloom

pp. 120–121: The year is 1978. . . . Goddess called Coyolxauhqui: Moctezuma and Hiser, 767.

pp. 121–122: By the 1400s . . . thirty-story building: Moctezuma and Hiser, 768.

p. 122: The Aztec worshipped . . . at least one god: Rojas, 127–28.

pp. 123–124: Although always . . . and builders: Koch, 138.

p. 124: Men mostly wore . . . scarlet: Davison, 199.

p. 125: At its height, the city of Tenochtitlán . . . inhabitants: Draper, Garrett, and Lopez, 132–33.

p. 126: The new advisors . . . he ordered killed: Koch, 134.

p. 127: To make glum matters gloomier . . . night sky: Koch, 141.

p. 128: "I implore you . . . gentlemen that accompany me": Loewen, 54.

p. 130: "with the castanets in its tail" :As quoted in Koch, 199.

p. 131: "excrement of the gods":As quoted in Koch, 80.

p. 131: According to Spanish . . . three days later: Rojas, 38.

p. 131 Many of them fell . . . sank like stones: Rojas, 71.

p. 124 [sidebar]: Players on the losing team . . . sacrificed: Koch, 143.

Chapter Fourteen: Grave Considerations

p. 134: Almost immediately . . . century coffin: Hansen and McGowan, 4–5.

p. 136: By 1626 . . . New Amsterdam tripled: Medford et al., 16.

p. 137: The British . . . enslaved Black people: Medford, Brown, and Carrington, 25.

p. 140: Some skeletons . . . have come from: Goodman et al., 105–7.

pp. 140–141: But then the British . . . side of the British: Dunmore; Countryman, 47.

p. 142: "dishonorable Violation of the public Faith": As quoted in Quarles, Tate, and Nash, 168.

p. 143: "fine boy," "likely rascal," and "nearly worn out.": Quarles, Tate, and Nash, 172.

p. 143: "I have discovered . . . never be restored.": As quoted in Quarles, Tate, and Nash, 169.

p. 144: No one is sure . . . 10,000 to 20,000 people: Rothstein.

p. 143 [sidebar]: by 1703 . . . enslaved Black people: Cantwell and Wall, 277–78.

Chapter Fifteen: Dead in a Ditch

p. 149: greasy, wild-goat . . . bread: MacIntyre.

p. 150: He was murdered: Owen.

pp. 151–152: Before his body . . . parts of skeletons: Cullen.

Chapter Sixteen: Skeleton Key

p. 155: Money pours . . . parking lot: Pitts, 86–87.

p. 155: The excavation . . . find Richard's grave: Pitts, 88.

p. 155: "not seriously considered possible.": Richard Buckley as quoted in "2012 Grey Friars Excavation."

p. 155: On the second day . . . the trenches: Pitts, 99.

p. 158: "lump of foul deformity": Shakespeare, *Richard III*, Act 1 Scene 2.

p. 158: In Shakespeare's day . . . deformed mind: "Myths and Legends."

p. 159: "laide openly . . . luke upon him,": As quoted in Pitts, 62, note 13.

p. 161: His diet was filled with . . . and heron: Rodriguez.

p. 161 [sidebar]: They compared ancient . . . their samples: King et al.

Chapter Seventeen: The Chamber of Secrets

p. 164: The two enter . . . slippery rocks: Shreeve.

p. 165: "Lee, you're really going to want to see this": Pedro Boshoff, as quoted in *Dawn of Humanity*.

p. 167: "Ph.D.'s and senior scientists . . . for pay": Berger and Hawks, 124–25; Bennett.

p. 168: "to see if I could make it through": Alia Gurtov (interview with author).

p. 169: "Once you were in there you didn't want to leave": Alia Gurtov (interview with author).

p. 170: The bones were transported . . . or feet: Wong, 2016.

p. 171: It's the largest . . . in Africa: Berger et al, "*Homo naledi*."

p. 171: After the specialists . . . and lighter: See Wong, 2017; Greshko; Shreeve.

p. 171: *H. naledi* had . . . way you do: Hendry.

p. 171: The bones . . . 335,000 years old: Dirks et al.

p. 172: Which raises yet . . . make fire?: Shreeve.

p. 173: At both sites . . . be uncovered: Hawks et al.

p. 173: The discoveries . . . questions: Zimmer.

p. 166 [sidebar]: Relative Terms: Blaxland.

Chapter Eighteen: You Don't Say

p. 176: A boy's skill . . . soldiers: Davison, 172.

p. 176: It was fashionable . . . the middle: Davison, 171.

p. 177: He took . . . "universal ruler": Man, 103.

p. 177: Over the next . . . of people: Frazier.

p. 179: If an arrow . . . arrow out: Lane, 31.

p. 180: Mongol warriors . . . dagger: Davison, 172.

p. 180: Heavy cavalrymen . . . hook: Lane, 31.

p. 181: Genghis Khan . . . blacksmiths: Man, 105.

p. 182: Riders traveled . . . food: Lane, 34.

p. 183: the Khan's corpse . . . of summer: Man, 257.

p. 183: And why kill . . . your path?: Man, 257.

p. 184: Streets, children . . . Mongolian money: Pocha.

p. 184: Mongolians don't . . . sacred places: Richmond.

p. 184: "virtual exploration system." . . . to look: McCoy.

p. 185: They haven't . . . investigation: Lin et al.

p. 180 [sidebar]: In peacetime . . . and mice: Davison, 171.

p. 180 [sidebar]: Mounted soldiers . . . eaten raw: Frazier.

A Little More Dirt on Archaeology

pp. 189–190: While archaeologists . . . background: D. Thomas, 244.

FURTHER READING

Berger, Lee R., and Marc Aronson. *The Skull in the Rock: How a Scientist, a Boy, and Google Earth Opened a New Window on Human Origins.* Washington, DC: National Geographic Children's Books, 2012.

Capek, Michael. *Unsolved Archaeological Mysteries.* North Mankato, MN: Capstone Press, 2015.

Cottman, Michael H. *Shackles from the Deep: Tracing the Path of a Sunken Slave Ship, a Bitter Past, and a Rich Legacy.* Washington, DC: National Geographic Children's Books, 2017.

Deem, James M. *Bodies from the Ash: Life and Death in Ancient Pompeii.* New York: Houghton Mifflin Harcourt, 2005.

———. *Faces from the Past: Forgotten People of North America.* Boston: Houghton Mifflin Harcourt, 2012.

Hollihan, Kerrie Logan. *Mummies Exposed! Creepy and True Series.* New York: Abrams Books for Young Readers, 2019.

Huey, Lois Miner. *American Archaeology Uncovers the Dutch Colonies.* New York: Marshall Cavendish Benchmark, 2010.

———. *American Archaeology Uncovers the Westward Movement.* New York: Marshall Cavendish Benchmark, 2010.

———. *Children of the Past: Archaeology and the Lies of Kids.* Minneapolis: Millbrook Press, 2017.

———. *Forgotten Bones: Uncovering a Slave Cemetery.* Minneapolis: Millbrook Press, 2016.

Macdonald, Fiona. *Amazing Archaeologists: True Stories of Astounding Archaeological Discoveries.* London: Raintree, 2015.

Rubalcaba, Jill, and Peter Robertshaw. *Every Bone Tells a Story: Hominin Discoveries, Deductions, and Debates.* Watertown, MA: Charlesbridge, 2010.

Scandiffio, Laura. *Digging Deep: How Science Unearths Puzzles from the Past.* Toronto, Ontario: Annick Press, 2019.

Schlitz, Laura Amy. *The Hero Schliemann: The Dreamer Who Dug for Troy.* Somerville, MA: Candlewick Press, 2013.

Walker, Sally M. *Written in Bone: Buried Lives of Jamestown and Colonial Maryland.* Minneapolis: Carolrhoda Books, 2009.

PLACES TO VISIT ONLINE OR IN PERSON

For a good summary of the archaeological process:
https://www.alexandriava.gov/historic/archaeology/default.aspx?id=33498.

For general information about archaeology, visit these two National Park Service sites:
https://www.nps.gov/archeology/public/kids/index.htm and https://www.nps.gov/efmo/learn/education/so-what-does-an-archeologist-do.htm.

See also "How You Can Become a Space Archaeologist" at National Geographic.com:
https://www.nationalgeographic.com/archaeology-and-history/archaeology/.

To make environmental observations that complement NASA satellite observations to help scientists studying Earth and the global environment, visit this NASA site:
https://observer.globe.gov/about/get-the-app.

Explore the African Burial Ground National Monument of New York City (at 290 Broadway) here:
http://www.nps.gov/afbg/index.htm.

To learn more about Ötzi the Iceman, housed in the South Tyrol Museum of Archaeology (in Bolzano, Italy):
www.iceman.it.

For the Ancient Egypt exhibit at the British Museum (Great Russell Street, London), visit:
http://www.ancientegypt.co.uk/menu.html.

To dive deep into the Antikythera Mechanism Research Project:
http://www.antikythera-mechanism.gr/.

Explore the Lascaux Cave:
http://archeologie.culture.fr/lascaux/en.

Learn more about the peoples of the Mesa Verde Region (including Folsom):
https://www.crowcanyon.org/EducationProducts/peoples_mesa_verde/intro.asp.

See this National Geographic blog for information on the Homo Naledi/Rising Star Expedition:
https://blog.nationalgeographic.org/tag/rising-star-expedition/.

For excavations in China, see:
http://archive.fieldmuseum.org/expeditions/china6_expedition/about.html.

For information about indigenous peoples, with a focus on British Columbia, go to the Simon Fraser University Museum of Archaeology and Ethnology:
http://www.sfu.ca/archaeology/museum/about.html.

For stories about women pioneers in archaeology, geology, and paleontology, go to Trowelblazers, created by four women scientists:
https://trowelblazers.com/about/.

For information about underwater archaeology, see the Museum of Underwater Archaeology website:
https://mua.apps.uri.edu/HTMLTEST/childrens.htm#bottom.

PHOTO CREDITS

Shutterstock; 83: Lytoke123456; 84: Ziko van Dijk; 85: Berthold Werner; 87: Dennis Jarvis; 90: Abrget47j; 91: ITV/Shutterstock; 92: Werner Forman Archive/Shutterstock; 96: Claude Valette; 97: Lennart Larsen/The Ancient of Denmark, National Museum of Denmark; 100: Santi Rodriguez/Shutterstock; 103: pavalena/ Shutterstock; 105: De Agostini/Biblioteca Ambrosiana/age fotostock; 111: Jmhullot; 113: incamerastock/Alamy Stock Photo; 115: GTW/imageBROKER/age fotostock; 117: Boiko Y/Shutterstock; 120: miguelão; 122: De Agostini Picture Library/age fotostock; 123 left: Icom Images/Alamy Stock Photo; 123 right: FLHC 76/Alamy Stock Photo; 126: The Print Collector/Getty Images; 127: The Picture Art Collection/Alamy Stock Photo; 130: Look and Learn/ Bridgeman Images; 135: The New York Public Library; 139: The New York Public Library; 141: Courtesy of the Library of Virginia; 146: South Tyrol Museum of Archaeology; 148: Thilo Parg/ Wikimedia Commons; 152: South Tyrol Museum of Archaeology; 154: Stefano Baldini/age fotostock; 157: PhotoFest; 158: Painters/ Alamy Stock Photo; 159: Sammy33/Shutterstock; 160: Georgios Kollidas/Shutterstock; 162: Gavin Fogg/AFP/GettyImages; 165: 2015, Berger et al.; 168: Simon Fraser University; 169: Robert Clark/National Geographic Creative; 170: Robert Clark/National Geographic Creative; 171: Cicero Moraes (Arc-Team); 175: GL Archive/Alamy Stock Photo; 178: Antiqua Print Gallery/Alamy Stock Photo; 179: Fine Art Images/age fotostock; 181: Fine Art Images/age fotostock; 183: AF archive/Alamy Stock Photo; 188: AF archive/Alamy Stock Photo.

ACKNOWLEDGMENTS

I am grateful to many people for their support, advice, and guidance with this book. Thanks to specialists and expert consultants Dr. David Hurst Thomas, Tom Blaber, and Anna Semon in the Division of Anthropology at the American Museum of Natural History; history teacher Victor Cuicahua; sculptor and art historian Mark Mennin; Dr. Alia Gurtov, Honorary Fellow in the Department of Anthropology at the University of Wisconsin, Madison; Dr. Brendan Haug, Assistant Professor of Classical Studies and Archivist of the Papyrology Collection, University of Michigan, Ann Arbor; Elizabeth Nabney, a PhD candidate at the University of Michigan, studying classical languages and literature; Dr. Jonathan Losos, professor in the Department of Biology at Washington University; David Anthone, Historic Preservation Officer, US General Services Administration; and Nancy J. Brighton, Deputy Federal Preservation Officer and Cultural Resources Community of Practice Lead, HQ, US Army Corps of Engineers.

Any errors are mine, and not those of my expert readers and consultants.

Thanks as well to Panita Prakittiphoom for her help with tracking down information for me in Bangkok about the Golden Buddha; to my writer friends and readers for reviewing the manuscript at multiple stages: Loree Griffin Burns, Melissa Stewart, April Jones Prince, Kate Narita, Kathryn Hulick, Erin Dionne, Nancy Werlin, Ammi-Joan Paquette, Michaela Muntean, Cassie Willson, and Jon

Willson; to my niece Dara Straussman for helping facilitate an important interview; and to Andy and Zelie Pforzheimer for lending me their beautiful NYC apartment for days on end to finish my research, interviews, and writing.

Thanks to all the librarians at the Taft School for helping me dig up facts and primary sources I never would have found otherwise, for tracking down articles in obscure academic journals, and for my dozens of interlibrary loan requests, with special thanks to Patti Taylor, Sean Padgett, Beth Lovallo, Betsy Barber, and Janet Kenney. Thanks as well to the many, many reference librarians—nonfiction writers' best friends—for their assistance, particularly those at Darien Public Library, Wesleyan University Library, Widener Library at Harvard University, the Library of Congress, and my home-away-from-home, the New York Public Library.

Ongoing thanks to all my Nerdy Book Club teacher and librarian friends for their infectious and boundless love for reading, and for putting books by us authors and illustrators into the hands of their students. We couldn't do this without you.

Thanks to my wonderful agent, Caryn Wiseman, and to the amazing team at Scholastic, including copy editor Joy Simpkins; art director Christopher Stengel, designer Kay Petronio, illustrator Nathan Hackett, sales and marketing, editorial director, Lisa Sandell, and thanks most especially to my keen-eyed and insightful editor, Amanda Shih.

ABOUT THE AUTHOR

Sarah Albee is the *New York Times* bestselling author of (mostly) nonfiction books for kids. Recent titles include *North America: A Fold-out Graphic History*; *Dog Days of History*; *Poison: Deadly Deeds, Perilous Professions, and Murderous Medicines*; and *Alexander Hamilton: A Plan for America*. Other nonfiction titles include *Why'd They Wear That?*; *Bugged: How Insects Changed History*; and *Poop Happened: A History of the World from the Bottom Up*. She lives in Connecticut with her husband, a high school history teacher and administrator, and their three children. You can learn more about Sarah and her books here: sarahalbeebooks.com.